SO-DYD-555

A PRACTICAL GUIDE TO SUCCESSFUL INTERVIEWING

A PRACTICAL GUIDE TO SUCCESSFUL INTERVIEWING

Philip Hodgson

McGRAW-HILL BOOK COMPANY

London · New York · St Louis · San Francisco · Auckland
Bogotá ·Guatemala · Hamburg · Lisbon · Madrid · Mexico
Montreal · New Delhi · Panama · Paris · San Juan
São Paulo · Singapore · Sydney · Tokyo · Toronto

Published by
McGRAW-HILL Book Company (UK) Limited
MAIDENHEAD · BERKSHIRE · ENGLAND

British Library Cataloguing in Publication Data

Hodgson, Philip.
A practical guide to successful interviewing.
1. Employment interviewing
I. Title
658.3'1124   HF5549.5.16

ISBN 0–07–084941–2

Library of Congress Cataloging-in-Publication Data

Hodgson, Philip.
Interviewing skills.
Includes index.
1. Employment interviewing.   I. Title.
HF5549.5.I6H58   1987   658.3'1124   87–3658

ISBN 0–07–084941–2

Contents

	Preface	vii
1.	Introduction	1
2.	Recruitment, selection and assessment	6
3.	The selection interview	21
4.	The appraisal interview	34
5.	The counselling interview	47
6.	The grievance interview	58
7.	The disciplinary interview	67
8.	Information giving and gathering	74
9.	Being an interviewee	83
	Index	93

Preface

This book emerged from a practical need. Although I knew that plenty had been written over the years on the subject of interviewing, I could not find much that was written from the manager's point of view rather than from some theoretical viewpoint. I was closely involved in training managers to develop their interviewing skills at the time, but could not find anything written recently to use as a practical guide. I decided to try to fill the gap myself, and this book is the result.

It is aimed at the manager who, as usual, is short of time but trying to do a good job. Most managers have had little training in interviewing skills, yet probably spend quite a proportion of their managerial lives in some kind of interview or other. I had it in mind that the manager would keep this book in the top drawer of the desk and skim through the appropriate chapter (or—if time is really short—just the checklist) before doing the interview. It is not meant to be a great academic tome. I have tried to cover the subject in sufficient depth to make the interview successful, but have tried to avoid too much detail.

My thanks go to Peter Drew and other editors at McGraw-Hill; to my colleagues at Ashridge Management College, many of whom were willingly badgered into reading sections of the book, giving advice, and offering ideas; and finally to my wife and children for their help, support and tolerance during the writing of the book.

Philip Hodgson
Ashridge Management College
September 1986

1
Introduction

This is a book on interviewing techniques. It is aimed at managers, supervisors and other people who have to interview or be interviewed as part of their everyday life. It has four aims:

1. To help managers to interview more effectively, even if they do not interview very often.
2. To cover a wide range of interview situations and give practical details of the skills and techniques required by the effective interviewer.
3. To provide a source of quick reference and checklists for the person who interviews occasionally.
4. To be relevant to managers from small, medium or large organizations, in the public or private sectors.

Content
The book has one chapter on each of a number of major kinds of interview. The interviews I have chosen are:

● Selection
● Appraisal
● Counselling
● Grievance
● Discipline
● Information giving and getting
● Being interviewed.

Each chapter is a self-contained unit. There are obviously overlaps, when content or style of two kinds of interview is similar. Chapters 3 and 9 have some overlap because they view the selection interview from two different angles—as the interviewer and as the interviewee.

At the end of each chapter there is an example of a real interview of the kind being discussed. It is presented as a script, and although none are verbatim accounts of actual conversations, I have tried to make each one as real as possible. No interview is perfect, but then real life is seldom perfect either. Each example provides an opportunity to review and comment on the various practical problems that a manager might encounter in doing that kind of interview.

What is an interview?

I suspect that many people think of an interview as something you have with the boss, and it's not always nice. My definition is very broad and covers a wide range of situations. It is: 'A conversation between two people which has a purpose.' This distinguishes the interview from, say, a casual chat, but does allow the word 'interview' to cover many of the conversations and meetings that a manager gets involved in on a day-to-day basis.

It is reported that junior and middle managers spend more than half their time talking to people, and that senior managers may spend up to 90 per cent of their time in the same way. Much of this communication falls into the category that I am calling interviewing. Managers trying to develop their communication skills would find it worth while spending some time improving their interviewing skills.

In all interviews there are four key skills that have to be applied. They are:

- Planning and preparing
- Listening and observing
- Questioning and probing
- Assessment and decision making.

Planning and preparing

Very few people get enough interviewing practice to be able to do first class interviews without preparation. Indeed, for several of the interviews described later, the only route to a good interview is through preparation. In my experience, managers give far too little time or effort to the planning and preparation stage of an interview. It should be no surprise that they do not get the results that they would like.

Actually the preparation stage may not take all that long, but it does have to be effective preparation. The aim is to have collected your thoughts as much as possible before you start the interview. Most infrequent interviewers have enough to do just keeping the interview going in the right direction; they don't have time to think up better ways of asking questions, or planning the interview. It therefore makes sense to do as much as possible beforehand. In the selection interview, for example, that preparation can range from deciding what sort of job it is and what sort of person you are looking for, to reading the application form in advance and making sure there are no interruptions. For an appraisal interview, preparation may involve deciding on the purpose of the interview. In the chapters that follow, preparation is stressed as vital.

Listening and observing

There is an old Chinese proverb which says:

'God gave you one mouth and two ears. Why don't you use them in that proportion?'

It is my belief that managers are generally very poor at listening. It is one of the skills that seems to be most needed but least valued. No interview should be a monologue, and that means the interviewee ought to have something to say. If, however, that interviewee gets the strong impression that whatever he or she says is merely taking up time before the interviewer can start talking again, then the interview will be a failure.

People send messages in all kinds of ways, and speech is only one method. The effective interviewer not only listens to what the interviewee says, but also learns to read the non-verbal signs as well. Posture, voice tone, eye contact, facial expression, and many other aspects of body language will all send messages. Sometimes those messages contradict the words that are being used. In most interviews, but in counselling especially, the ability to observe and interpret those messages is most useful.

Questioning and probing

Question technique is very important in all interviews. It may be a matter of asking the right question at the right time. It may be a way of getting a useful answer in 30 seconds rather than the same answer in 5 minutes. All because of the way you used questions. Anyone can find out something about someone in 3 hours, but the skilled interviewer finds out the same amount in 30 minutes by using questions effectively.

Questions fall into three major categories:

1. *Open questions.* The aim is to get the interviewee talking and open up the subject. Generally they cannot be answered by yes or no.

They usually start with What, Why, How, Tell; for example, What do you think of office automation? Why do you want to leave this company? Tell me about your work in America.

2. *Closed questions.* These questions narrow down to something specific. They can be answered with a yes or no or another single word. Used for checking facts and clarifying, they usually start with Do, Have, Will, Where; for example, Where were you on the night of the fourteenth? Do you speak French? Have you ever managed an office?

3. *Hypothetical questions.* Used to test some possibility or to review competence, these questions can be difficult to phrase without giving away the answer you would like to hear. They generally include the word if: How would you cope if. . . ? If that happened to you . . . ? How would you cope if our competitors reduced their price by 15 per cent? If everyone were treated like that what would happen?

In each of the following chapters questioning technique is reviewed and suggestions are made to increase both efficiency and effectiveness.

Assessment and decision making
All interviews have a purpose, and that purpose is often concerned with some decision (selection) or some subsequent action (appraisal, grievance). Methods of decision making are out of the scope of this book, but the criteria by which you make those decisions are part of the preparation, and are reviewed in each chapter. Sometimes (Information giving and gathering) you have to start an interview without knowing precisely what it is you are looking for. However, even in these cases it is possible to decide on what would have to happen to make the interview a success or what would have to happen to make it a failure.

In the chapter on selection, a lot of emphasis is put on describing the job to be done and the person you feel would best fit into that job. Other methods of assessment are described too, because although the interview is still the most popular selection method, there are a variety of others which ought to be considered.

Style and control
The style that is used during the interview will depend on both interviewer and interviewee and on the kind of interview that is being conducted. Interviewers have to find and develop a style that suits them

and adapt it to the various situations that may arise. One of the main aspects of style is the degree of control that interviewers wish to maintain over the interview. Some interviewers will be quite happy to let the interviewee talk at length, others will want to use more closed questions and keep things moving on a tighter rein. Personally I don't think there are many wrongs or rights in this area. It is very subjective, and fortunately there are lots of ways of interviewing effectively. The only thing that doesn't seem to work is to try to adopt someone else's style. The gaps always show.

A few words about sex and discrimination
I wanted this book to apply to all managers, and therefore did not want to use the male or female pronoun for every example. I found putting 'he or she' very cumbersome, and impossible in the scripted examples, so I decided to alternate the use of male and female managers and interviewees throughout.

Apart from the moral considerations, in the chapter on selection I have argued strongly against discrimination of any sort on managerial grounds. Quite a lot of research is currently looking at how women are perceived by men at selection interviews. Appearance, voice tone, eye contact and degree of assertiveness are some of the many areas of possible misinterpretation when relating the interview to job performance. There are so many vested interests, and so much cultural conditioning, that rapid change is unlikely, but I hope that none of my examples are seen as backward.

2
Recruitment, selection and assessment—the preparation stage

Selecting someone for a job is probably the single biggest opportunity that managers have to influence the development of their organization for good or ill. Ask yourself this question: How much will it cost my company in one year if I make a bad choice rather than a good one? A brief example will demonstrate the point.

Assume that the person you are recruiting is going to stay with your organization for a number of years, and during that time they are going to make decisions involving company resources. For the sake of illustration, assume that if you make a 'good' decision the person will be 10 per cent better at using those resources than an average sort of candidate. So if the good person is buying things they will spend 10 per cent less, if they are selling things they will earn 10 per cent more, and so on. Also assume that if you make a 'bad' decision the person you end up with will be 10 per cent worse than the average. Now, how much is a 'good' person worth compared to a 'bad' one? When I ask this question of the managers I meet, I get answers ranging from a few hundred pounds per year up to the truly staggering one million pounds per year! Of the other resources at stake, time seems to be the next most often quoted, with estimates of potential losses ranging between one week and six months.

Of course, you can prove anything with figures, and I wouldn't want to suggest that the calculations described above are anything other than very rough estimates. But they do illustrate the potential of the decision that is made every time a person is appointed to a job. The true cost of making the appointment is itself quite steep. It includes advertising when recruiting from outside the company and involves a lot of hidden costs like administration and training. True costs of recruiting have been estimated in tens of thousands of pounds. By and large, it seems a good idea, if you are involved in selection or recruitment, to do your best to get it right. Now let's look at what is involved.

The vacancy
You're unlikely to be recruiting someone unless there is something for them to do, and somewhere for them to do it. In most organizations you start with a vacancy, either because someone is leaving or because a new job needs to be done. At this stage it is worth spending a little time deciding if there is a need to fill the vacancy at all. Sometimes the decision is made for you, and in the last few years many managers will have received a memo putting a block on all outside recruitment while this or that cost-cutting exercise goes on. Economic pressures are probably the most common reason for an organization to stop recruiting, but that shouldn't mean that some of the other alternatives to recruitment cannot be considered. An enormous number of organizations have been through major reorganizations and without doubt these have generated opportunities to get work done without the need to fill all the vacancies that have occurred. You may be sick of reorganizations, but it may still be a worthwhile alternative to just replacing like with like.

Other alternatives to recruitment might include the secondment or transfer of someone from within the organization. It might be worth considering whether temporary or contract staff could provide the service you need. It might even be worth while contracting the work out completely. Of course for some kinds of job, computer-based automation may offer alternative prospects for handling the work. Just a word of caution here. In my experience, both manufacturing and office automation tend to end up needing the same number of bodies on the payroll. The difference is that before automation you employed a lot of people with manual skills to keep output going—which the automation replaced—and after automation you need a lot of people with computer skills to keep the computer going. I suppose in the end we will get more computers to keep the computers going, but by that time this kind of book will be written by computer anywaywaywaywaywayway.

Once you have established that the vacancy needs to be filled, and the work can't be dealt with in any other way, you set out to select someone for the job. You need to decide whether you are going to look inside or outside the organization, or both. Many organizations have union agreements or personnel policies which will affect what you can do and how you do it. Companies with personnel departments will probably expect their personnel staff to be involved in the selection process. For the rest of this chapter, I'm going to assume that our manager will be looking both inside and outside the company and, although being helped by the personnel department, will still be involved in every stage of the process.

Describe the job

Before you can go out and select someone, you need to know what sort of person you are looking for; and before you can really decide that you have to be sure what sort of job you want them to do. This is not heady stuff, it is stunningly basic, but I am frequently horrified by the haphazard way in which managers fail to be clear on what work is to be done and how and what leeway there is for change. To start with, are you aiming to replace the previous job holder with someone who will do the same or are you actually expecting the person to take the job into new areas? (For example, when the previous job occupant was with you, she was talented at presenting ideas to quite senior audiences—as it wasn't one of your areas of particular strength you encouraged her. Does this mean that the job responsibilities should now include making presentations to senior customers?)

An important place to start is with the exit interview. When a person is about to leave a job—especially if they are about to leave the company—they are more likely to feel able to talk frankly about the work they have been doing, the potential it has for the future, and why they really wanted to leave. Exit interviews are an excellent source of information on which to base your planning for filling the next job. So let us assume that either you or the personnel people have conducted an exit interview and that there are one or two lessons to be learned from it. Next, you have to decide how much the new job is to be like the old one. It may be that the previous job holder had been operating in a very fixed routine with little room for development or flexibility. Perhaps those routines had become formalized into a job description. Do you now want to make some structural changes to the job? You might want to consider changes in responsibility levels, in allocation of tasks, or in the measurement of performance or results.

Having looked at the possibilities, you ought to be able to draft a job description, or, at the very least, amend the one you already have in the filing cabinet. Don't forget that any job description will get out of date, and if you are in an organization that is going through a lot of change, then it is likely that the job description you had even a year ago has little to do with the job that needs to be done now. Different companies and different managers tend to write job descriptions in different ways. Some will talk about aims and objectives, others will talk about the tasks and activities that have to be done. Some will include performance measures and targets, others will give no indication about how performance is measured, if indeed it is measured at all.

During the last few years many organizations have adopted much more flexible methods of operating and managing their businesses to meet the changing needs of their markets. In companies like these the job description may seem to be as much use as a blank sheet of paper. Certainly the old style of 'cast-in-stone' job description would be of very little use. However, even in the most 'flexible' companies, people need to know what they are trying to achieve. Some indication of the purpose of the job, together with key areas of responsibility and authority, are essential if the person doing that job is to have any chance of success. It is also essential if you are to have any chance of selecting the right person for the job.

Describe the person
Having described the job that you want done in language that is appropriate to your organization, you now need to describe the person you are looking for. There are lots of ways of doing this and you must find the way that suits you. The important thing is to decide before you start on what you want. If you don't then your selection strategy will be forced down to the level of the impulse buyer and frankly you might as well save yourself the bother of arranging an interview and just use a pin on the list of applicants.

How do you describe the person you are looking for? I find that dividing the description up into three chunks works well. It means asking three key questions, each beginning with the word what:

- *What can they do?* The skills and experience that a person would bring to the job.
- *What are they like?* Their personality and the way they behave.
- *What do they want?* Their expectations of the job, including what motivates them.

What can they do? Skills and experience
If you are selecting someone to fly an aeroplane then it is probably a

good idea if they have a pilot's licence. If you are looking for a salesperson then it would be useful if they had experience in selling. At this sort of level, working out what skills a person needs is straightforward and easy.

However, with most jobs and certainly with most people, there are lots of grey areas. It is useful therefore to divide up those skills that you see as relevant to the work into three more categories. They are:

- *Essential* Those skills, or levels of skill which are absolutely crucial to the work. For a salesperson these skills might include talking to people face to face and a good telephone manner.
- *Desirable* It would be nice if the candidate possessed these skills, but they are not entirely essential. Perhaps they could be taught to the person soon after arrival in the organization. Taking our sales example again, it would be nice if the person had a working knowledge of our particular product range, but that could be taught. Knowledge of the general market, however, would be seen as essential.
- *Disqualifiers* Something that would in some way prevent the person from being given further consideration. A salesperson who had a poor driving record, or who was currently without a driving licence, might be one example. There might also be safety implications. For instance, colour blindness could be a hazard in some kinds of jobs.

Draw up a chart of what skills and experience you feel you are looking for in the right person for the job. Think through whether those skills are essential, desirable, or disqualifiers. Now, if you have time (and in my view it is time well spent) show your list to one or two colleagues in the organization. They may have some useful suggestions to make about some of the skills you have listed. It may be that you have understated the level of experience needed for the work. In that case a lot of early training is going to be needed before the new person is really able to pull their weight. It may be that you have overestimated the skills level required. Not many years ago it was felt that only university graduates were able to take on the task of writing computer programmes. Quite rightly that view has now changed, and a lot of very able programmers who were previously excluded from the market have been able to show their ability.

There is one final aspect to consider under the heading of skills and experience. It is not easy to describe, but is just as essential to ensure that the candidate you select is going to be effective in your organization. The question you need to ask is: 'What kind of person will fit into our kind of business?' A brilliant track record with your competitors is not necessarily a guarantee of success with you. Research over the last few years has suggested that at management level there is no such thing as the 'good' manager. Instead you have to talk about the good manager in this or that particular environment or culture. How similar are the cultures? How do you describe culture? It's not easy, since very few organizations are conscious of having a culture at all, let alone how it differs from that of another company. Areas like autonomy, performance standards, urgency, attention to detail, are all important in different ways in different organizations.

Nowadays, with legislation covering many aspects of the selection process, the manager has to be careful not to break the law unwittingly. In my view discrimination against any part of the population is bad management—quite apart from the moral issues involved. If you are genuinely trying to select the best candidate for the job, then it makes no managerial sense to eliminate some of the candidates before you ever look at their abilities. However, there is also a kind of catch-22 here. After all, what is selection if it isn't discrimination? In making an appointment you are choosing one from a group of many. How do you do that without discriminating? The answer to that one is not easy. It seems to me that the difference is between your own personally held biases, and some general issues of performance related to the job in question.

What are they like? Personality

At the same time as you are finding out what a person can do, and what experience they have, you are also finding out what the person is like. The word personality is often used here—perhaps I should say misused. I still hear people saying things like 'She has a good personality', or 'We want a person with lots of personality'. To the speaker, these statements make some sense, but to anyone else they can only be meaningless. The problem is that no one is ever going to see or directly measure someone's personality. All you can do is to make some guesses about personality based on what the person does and how they act. In other words, it is only the behaviour that you can measure; the personality remains hidden forever. So what can you do?

First of all bear in mind that the behaviour you are seeing at the beginning of the interview may not be typical of the person when they are relaxed and in surroundings that are familiar. Most people find interviews somewhat stressful, and stress often affects our behaviour. So unless you have a particular need to observe the person under stress—and even then be sure it is the same kind of stress that you want to simulate—it is worth while trying to help them relax during the interview. This will be covered in more detail in the section on the interview itself.

What do you need to know about the person's personality? Ask any two psychologists, and they will probably disagree on what are the essentials of personality. Any number of personality tests (or inventories, if you want to be up-market) have been designed over the last few decades, and many are very reliable and useful. However, there is no currently accepted standard. Although personality tests can be of enormous use in helping to make a selection, there are some major traps that the unwitting user can fall into. I would strongly advise anyone contemplating the use of tests for the first time to get professional advice.

I have chosen four areas of personality that, to me, seem to be worth considering when drafting a person specification.

1. *How outgoing is the person?* Do they spend most of their time with other people, or do they tend to do things on their own? Evidence for this might be from hobbies and sports—team sports are an obvious indicator, but even if the person says their hobby is fell walking, it may be that they organize group outings and spend most of their time walking in groups. Being outgoing may not be an advantage. The job may be one which requires spending a long time at, say, a computer terminal. In this instance it may be a positive advantage to have someone who does not mind spending long periods without talking to other people. For a sales job, where meeting new people is a major part of the work, the outgoing type is much more likely to be successful.

2. *How much does the person want to control things?* How dominant are they? Have they tended to lead or follow others in their life so far? In the interview with you, have they disagreed with you, cut across you while you were talking, and perhaps even tried to direct the flow of the interview? All these are signs that the person in front of you wants to control the circumstances around them. It's neither a good nor a bad thing, but do remember that it will strongly affect how that person does the job, and how effectively they will work with you.

3. *How much warmth does the person show to you?* (Or to anybody else

that you have seen them with?) For some kinds of job, it is essential that the person is able to establish a good working relationship quickly with colleagues, customers, clients, patients, etc. On the other hand a different kind of job may require a more cool, detached, logical approach, where too close an involvement with some people may prejudice effective decisions.

4. *To what extent does the person want to change what is already done?* Some people tend to want to do things differently, other people tend to want to take what is already there and modify it to make it work better in some way. This tendency will probably affect how your candidate makes decisions, and copes with change. In an organization in which lots of changes are being made, it may be useful to have someone who has lots of new ideas. However, for every person with a new idea there need to be quite a few modifiers around to take that idea and actually make it work.

These few notes on personality are suggestions only. The study of personality, and what makes one person different from another, has been going on for centuries, and is still only in its infancy. My suggestions are incomplete, and if pushed too far can probably be made to appear contradictory. But with all aspects of selection, if you don't know what you are looking for, how will you recognize it when it arrives? Form your own views on what sort of person you are looking for, describe them in words that make sense to you and then devise ways of attracting that person, and recognizing them at the interview.

What do they want? Expectations

You may say that until you ask them, how on earth can you expect to know what your candidate might want. However, there are a number of points that you could anticipate. The most obvious is pay. Presumably you, or someone in your organization, has checked what comparable jobs are earning elsewhere. If not then you could be overwhelmed or very disappointed by the response you get to your advertisement. Other areas might be career progression, hours of work, closeness to facilities, housing or transport. A job which involves travelling the country and staying away from home is probably not going to suit someone who has domestic or other ties to where they live. A graduate entrant may be interested in future job opportunities and management training, and less concerned about the immediate job they would come into. For people in middle age, transferability of pension fund might be important. And, of course, with redundancies a regular part of business life, the growth and stability of the company is likely to be of interest to all.

When you are describing the person, remember that they will have some expectations about the company as well, and if you can anticipate those expectations you will have a better chance of attracting the right person.

Attract some candidates

Strictly speaking this part is nothing to do with interviewing at all. However, many managers get involved with the process, so I am including it for the sake of completeness.

The aim is quite simple: to get a few applications of the right calibre from which to make a final selection. There are four ways of getting applications:

- Advertise
- Head-hunt
- Grapevine
- Unsolicited letters.

Advertise

Recruitment advertising is a skill and a science in itself. There are fads and fashions, and unless you are able to keep up to date on a day-to-day basis, my strong suggestion is that you get some external help with any major project. While unemployment stays high, some jobs will attract a heavy response; but certain skills stay in short supply and require competitive advertising.

If you do find yourself composing an advert, remember that potential customers may also be reading it, and there are some good public relations to be won or lost by what you say and how you say it. The ideal advert attracts only a few good candidates, and that may mean telling people about the tough parts of the job as well as the attractive bits. A famous example of this appeared in *The Times* at the turn of the century:

> Men wanted for hazardous journey. Small wages, bitter cold, long months of complete darkness, constant danger, safe return doubtful. Honour and recognition in case of success.
>
> (Sir) Edward Shackleton 1900

Head-hunt

Head-hunting has grown tremendously over the last ten years. A lot of consultants now specialize in just this kind of recruitment, and for some jobs it is a worthwhile option. Companies tend to use head-hunters when there are only a limited number of people who might be good enough to do the job, or it might be that the organization does not wish to tell the world that it is looking for a key member of staff. It may not even want its existing employees to know that job changes are likely, although in my view this is bad management and a poor reason for using a head-hunter. The head-hunter will do all the preliminary work and will produce a shortlist of suitable candidates for you to select from. Of course, you only get what you ask for and it is part of the skill of the head-hunter to help you specify precisely what it is you do want. Even though you might not initiate it, you will probably be taken through similar questions to the ones I was putting to you in the previous section. There really is no escape from that stage of the exercise!

Head-hunters can provide a comprehensive service, and you must expect to pay for it. But if you want the bulk of the preparation work done for you, or if confidentiality is important, then you should at least consider the head-hunter. Remember that some will charge for every candidate that they bring to you, so be clear before you start on how the bill will mount up. Also remember, if you are head-hunted yourself, that the head-hunter is working for the employer and not for you, so don't let a smooth bedside manner make you believe otherwise.

Grapevine
The grapevine is probably one of the oldest methods known for passing and receiving messages. Within a company it probably still accounts for a lot of job placements. In some business sectors, or particular groupings of professionals where there is a wide network of contacts, the grapevine can be expected to reach quite a high percentage of the people who might be interested and capable of doing the job. The 'old-boy' network is the one most commonly referred to, and a very good system it is too—so long as you are part of the network. If you are outside the net, then of course it is discriminatory, blinkered and élitist.

For the sake of getting the best person for the job, it makes sense to get the message to as wide a group of people as possible, so if you are tempted to use networks I would strongly suggest that you employ some other method as well. Having assembled a variety of applicants, select on merit and not on which family, school, college, regiment or whatever the person comes from.

Unsolicited letters

The personnel department and the managing director will be receiving these all the time. The era of the professional cv writer is upon us and, coupled with the power of wordprocessing and easily available mailing lists, we can expect an increase in such delights. A large percentage of the letters arriving will be of no value, but if your organization is well known for employing certain specialist skills, then it may be worth giving the unsolicited letters a quick glance. Better still get someone else to sort them, and only look at the hopefuls.

If you are currently looking for a job, and are sending out letters, don't despair, but do expect a very low response rate. Your letter is competing with a lot of others, and anything that you can do to make it distinctive and attractive to that particular company is worth considering.

Choosing candidates

You have attracted a group of applicants, and you now have to make a selection from them. Armed with your job description and your person specification you have now to work out how best to recognize the ideal candidate when you see them.

You will probably break the selection process down into several stages. Your advertising should have been the first stage of selection. You may now be expecting to produce a shortlist, before going on to make a final decision. So far, we have assumed that although you have consulted other people, you will have taken the major decisions about person and job specifications yourself. Now you need to ask yourself who else needs to be involved in the selection process. There may be colleagues, bosses, technical experts, and lots of other people who will have to work with the person finally selected, and who will have views on how the decision should be made. Unless you involve them in some way at this stage, your leave yourself wide open to criticism if they subsequently don't like your final choice.

Also ask yourself who actually makes the final decision? Is it you? Does your boss have to approve the choice, and is this a rubber stamp or could that person turn your number one choice down? Who can make an offer of a job? Who will draft the contract, or make any modifications to the standard one? You need to know all this before you see your first candidate.

Shortlists and screening

If you have too many possible candidates, and will need to reduce the number to a manageable size, then you will have to find some way to screen and eliminate some of them.

A good application form will be of great use at this stage. I don't think it is worth while ploughing through vast numbers of interviews only to eliminate half the candidates for reasons that were obvious from the application form. In my view it is better to eliminate as many as possible on the basis of the application form. Then you can leave yourself enough time to make a thorough review of the last few candidates.

I have heard it argued that there is sometimes a need to see certain candidates for public relations reasons. This is often the case when internal applicants are being considered. The internal person is not reckoned to be suitable for the job, but would be embarrassed or demotivated if not given an interview. In these cases I think it is important to avoid giving a token interview. If the person wants to be considered for the job, and you feel you have to see them, then by all means interview—but make sure it is a proper interview. Ask the same questions, at the same level of difficulty, as you would all the other candidates. It might help this candidate to realize that perhaps this job wasn't for them, and in a few cases you might be surprised at the quality of the answers that you get.

But back to the screening. If you find that you still can't reduce the numbers of candidates enough on the basis of the application form, then you are going to have to find some other way of cutting the numbers. In Germany, for example, applicants' handwriting is sometimes analysed by a graphologist and predictions made about how they would cope with the job. I don't see it catching on very much in Britain, but a lot of organizations are organizing some kind of assessment day for their school-leaver and graduate recruitment. The aim of this is to review a lot of candidates, and to produce a shortlist from which offers will be made. Assessment centre methods have been growing in popularity over the last ten years and will be covered in the next section.

Selection methods

The interview is by far the most common method used by managers for recruitment and selection. Because it is so important, I am giving it a chapter to itself. The remainder of this chapter is about other selection methods and the follow-up process to making a selection. If your main concern is the selection interview please go on to the next chapter.

Panel interviews

In this book all of the interviews described involve two prime participants, the interviewer and the interviewee. However, some organizations use more than one interviewer. The skills of interviewing are just the same with a panel interview as they are with the single interviewer, but the members of the panel need to have one more skill— they need to listen to each other. Because of this the panel interview is often harder to do well. Panel members can easily get in each other's way, ask each other's questions and generally make the whole process less efficient than the single interviewer. The advantages are that several people get a look at the candidate, and while one panel member is asking a question, another can be thinking ahead to the next question.

The well-practised panel can work very effectively, and support each other very well. This is the secret of good panel interviewing. Try to work with panel members frequently so that you can operate like a team, not like a number of individuals struggling to grab some attention.

Tests and inventories

Tests fall into two broad categories: tests of ability or aptitude and tests designed to reveal personality. Computer programming aptitude tests are quite widely used to assess the chances that a person may turn out to be a good programmer even without previous experience. There are aptitude and ability tests for manual dexterity, filing, mental arithmetic, typing and a wide range of other skills. The important thing with each one is to be clear precisely what skill you want to test for.

Tests of personality come in an enormous variety of types. Some will have been developed for groups of people unlike those you want to use them on (i.e., the mentally ill), so it is worth being cautious about interpreting the results (and see my remarks on p. 12). However, personality is important for so many jobs that any help you can get in describing the differences between one candidate and another is, in my view, worth taking.

When buying a test, make sure that the test's designers or publishers are able to give you some kind of statistical data on reliability and validity. Validity is whether the test measures what it claims to measure, reliability is whether it does so every time. If statistics make you go weak at the knees, then find someone who can review the data for you. Otherwise you may find yourself with wonderful looking results that are absolutely meaningless.

Exercises and case studies
These are often a development of the idea of testing ability or aptitude. If you know that recruits will have to be able to read a balance sheet from day one, then it might be worth giving them a balance sheet and asking them to explain it to you. This simple idea can extend to quite complex case studies. A frequently used example is an in-tray exercise. Here the candidate is given a set of papers which would be found in the in-tray of the person who gets the job being advertised. The candidate has to take action, draft replies, make decisions, etc., on the basis of the information provided. A time limit is often imposed to see how the candidate will prioritize the time available.

Other exercises might be the assessment of a company's financial results, or drafting a marketing proposal for a new product. The general principle is to simulate the kind of problem that the successful candidate would have to face on taking up the new job.

Assessment centres
An assessment centre is merely the use of a variety of selection methods to try to improve the chances of making a better decision. Assessment centres often include psychological tests, exercises and simulations, group discussions (from which it is possible to see how a candidate deals with a group of people), presentations (where the candidate is asked to present some ideas to an audience), and one or more interviews.

An assessment centre usually involves several assessors, who evaluate each candidate on each selection exercise. At the end of the event, the assessors pool their results to make a final evaluation of each candidate.

The advantage of this method of assessment is that it gives a much fuller picture of each candidate than any single selection method, and thus helps the selectors to make a better decision. The method also involves several people in the assessment stage, which is useful if several managers are likely to be working with the successful candidate. The disadvantage is that it is costly in terms of money and time. I would argue that in a lot of cases the adoption of assessment centre methods is well worth the extra cost, since the cost of making a poor decision will be a lot higher.

Preparation stage: summary checklist

1. Consider alternatives to recruitment.
2. Describe the job.
3. Describe the person:
   - (a) Skills and experience
     Personality
     Expectations
   - (b) Essential
     Desirable
     Disqualifiers
4. Attract some candidates:
   Advertise
   Head-hunt
   Grapevine
   Unsolicited letter
5. Other selection methods:
   Panel interview
   Tests and inventories
   Exercises and case studies
   Assessment centres.

3
The selection interview

The interview is the most common method used to make selection decisions. Interviewing is a skill, and like any skill it is possible to learn to do it competently and consistently. A few people have a natural talent and without any training can interview brilliantly, and make reliable decisions. Most of us don't fall into that category but, because we have spent a fair proportion of our lives in talking to people, we quite naturally believe that we are good at it.

A good interview is a conversation with a clear purpose. What we often don't notice when comparing our everyday conversations to an interview is that, in everyday conversations, we very often don't know what the purpose is before we start. Unfortunately selection interviews often go wrong for the same reason. The interviewer, and sometimes the candidate, don't know what the purpose of the meeting is. In the previous chapter we spent a lot of time working out what kind of job it was that you were trying to fill, and what kind of person you were looking for to fill it. If at this moment you are waiting to start an interview, and you haven't thought through those two important points, then here is a suggestion:

● Tell the candidate that there will be a delay of ten minutes, make sure that the interviewee has some coffee, and then get out a sheet of paper. Turn back to the middle of Chapter 2 and jot down what the job is about and what kind of person you are looking for. With only eight minutes available it won't be a work of art, but at least it will help you with the next part. The other two minutes are spent on the interview plan. Unless you have a plan, you cannot be sure that the interview will cover all the essential areas that need to be raised. But let us hope that life isn't always going to be lived in this fire-fighting fashion.

If we were giving ourselves the right amount of time to do the job properly, what would help us do our interviewing in a professional way?

There are three stages in making the interview work well:

- The interview plan
- The circumstances
- The interview itself

The first two must happen before the interview takes place. Let us look at each of them in order.

The interview plan

Some people go for a fixed plan. They will have worked out perhaps ten questions that they will ask in the same order. Personally, I don't like that level of rigidity. I'm all in favour of identifying a number of areas which need to be covered, and probably some specific questions that need to be answered, but that still gives you some flexibility. Let us assume that you have shortlisted candidates as the result of seeing their application form and now you are planning the interview.

Typically the areas that you will wish to cover are going to be those identified in your person specification. The way to get at the information you need will be by asking about:

- School and job history, and relevant experience
- Outside interests
- Hypothetical examples.

You will have looked through the application form or cv and have noticed some aspects of the person's experience that suggests that they might be able to do the job. There might also have been one or two aspects that weren't clear, or that raised a question or doubt in your mind. For instance, the candidate has all the right experience, but has changed jobs four times in the last six years. There may be a number of perfectly good reasons why this is the case. Or it may be that this person gets bored easily. Or it may be that eighteen months is about the time it took most of those companies to find out how poor a performer the person really was! So in going through the information you have, try to piece together the jigsaw puzzle of what you know, what you need, and what you have to find out.

Although I use the application form as my guide when planning the interview, I do try to avoid reading out long chunks of it to candidates.

This really is a waste of everyone's time. After all, they wrote it, so they don't need it read back out loud. It is also a compliment to interviewees to show that you have read their form and can ask questions based on it. If there is information that needs to be checked, then of course do so, but otherwise try not to use the interview for things that could perfectly well have been done from the paperwork alone.

The hypothetical question is commonly used in selection interviews, and is sometimes the only possible way of covering certain ground. It is a difficult method to use because it is quite easy to unintentionally give away what you think is the right answer. The canny candidate will be quick to feed back your own ideas to you. Now most of us believe that people who have the sense to think like us are generally all right. Hence the danger, because we are not testing the candidates' thinking or reasoning skills, merely their ability to rephrase what we have just said. If you want to test how a candidate would respond to a particular situation, think it through beforehand and, in this case only, prepare a script, to make sure that each candidate gets the same problem.

Having drawn up your detailed plan, go back over it to estimate timescales. If you are doing several interviews in a day, you will need to keep a fairly close eye on the time. Nine interviews each losing ten minutes, adds up to an hour and a half at the end of the day. In this sort of situation, it will help you to keep track of how things are going if you have some idea of how long you want to spend on each stage of your plan. Remember to allow time for questions at the end. Having drawn up your plan, it is important to check the circumstances in which the interview will take place.

The circumstances
Before we look at interview methods, there are a number of administrative matters that need to be taken care of. If you don't think ahead in this way you will be reducing the chances of having a good interview, and you may well be signalling to the candidate that you don't really care.

No interruptions
This aspect is easier if you have a secretary, but even if you don't then it should be possible to take the phone off the hook, put a 'do not disturb' notice on the door, tell people who might call in that you are interviewing, etc. If you don't have your own office, or it's never safe from interruption, then find somewhere that is. If necessary, hire a room in a hotel down the road.

Clear desk

You should be signalling to candidates that the only thing on your mind during the interview is the interview. If your desk is knee-deep in papers, files, coffee cups and little bits of paper with URGENT written in red capitals, then candidates might just get the impression that they haven't got your full attention. They might find amusement in trying to read upside-down the most interesting looking memos on your desk.

Room layout and seating

Some people find a desk between them and the candidate is a barrier. Others find a desk is a reassurance. I think you have to find a style that suits you. Personally, I prefer an informal style and come out from behind my desk and, ideally, like to sit in armchairs around a coffee table. This may not be possible and it certainly won't suit everyone. But try not to put the candidate at a disadvantage by sitting them lower than you, or facing a sunny window.

I know of one interviewer who would put two chairs out for a candidate to choose from. One was comfortable but well away from the desk, the other was hard and upright, but conveniently situated by his desk. He would make candidates walk down the length of his (long) office and force them to choose where to sit. He felt he could tell something about the person's character by this device. In my view all it did was to tell candidates that the interviewer was going to play games with them throughout the interview and therefore lost any possibility of establishing a good rapport.

Coffee, smoking and other personal comforts

Offer candidates a drink, but do give them somewhere to put the cup down. Very often people are nervous at interviews and their hands will be just that little bit less steady. It's bad for them and for you if they sit with cups, saucers and spoons rattling away. If you smoke, offer them a cigarette, if you don't and you'd like them not to smoke during the interview, tell them so, but don't leave them in mid-air trying to guess. When people are nervous they may need to visit the toilet more frequently. Make sure that when they arrive someone tells them where the facilities are.

Timing

It is a courtesy and reflects on your managerial competence to keep to the times you have set the candidates. However, for whatever reason, you will sometimes run late. If this is the case you owe it even more to the people waiting outside to keep them informed about what is happening. It may be that they can go off and do something else, it may be that you can call people before they set out and advise them to delay. Whatever it is, you must be seen to be concerned and doing your best to minimize the time that is wasted. Remember that one of these people might become one of your staff, and they will not want to work for you if they feel you can waste their time in such a cavalier fashion.

The interview
You have a plan and you know that there are a number of areas that you wish to find out more about. The candidate has just come into the room and sat down. You have done the usual pleasant remarks, so what do you say to start the event?

Explain the purpose
Start by telling each candidate what is going to happen, what your expectations are, who else they are going to see, and how long you estimate the whole thing will last. If you like you can outline your interview plan as well, perhaps in the following way: 'I'd like to ask you some questions about yourself and your background, and then I will tell you something about the company, and answer any questions that you may have.'

On your interview plan you will have marked up the areas that you want to find out more about, and what you now need to do is to find a way of covering those points in a way that keeps the conversation flowing reasonably naturally. As I said in the section on the interview plan, I personally dislike having a fixed set of questions to be asked. However, I will probably start off each interview in the same way, and spend some time on the person's school or first job experience. My aim is to give candidates some fairly easy questions to start with to help them relax, and also to find out about their earliest school or job choices.

Use of questions
Open questions are important at this stage, with many follow-up clarifying questions. I want to get the candidate talking, and happy to expand on some topics. My job is to listen and steer the conversation with as few words as possible. Later on we will come to parts of the job history that need to be probed in more depth. I will ask more closed and

probing questions to cover the areas about which I was not clear. I will probe until I have resolved the query. My belief is that, by setting an early pattern in the interview of getting the candidate to talk freely, when we get to the harder probing bits, it will be easier for the candidate to tell me honestly the information that I need in order to make my selection decision.

Style and control
It will be apparent from the previous section that I prefer a fairly relaxed style. I set out the room to reflect this and during the interview I try to help candidates relax and give them opportunities to show their best. I'm quite happy to let candidates have quite a lot of control in the interview, if they are giving me information I need and not taking too long over it. One technique that can work quite well is at some stage to turn the interview round and ask candidates to interview you. This can be very effective, but it can also be a major time-waster, so only do it if you feel confident that you can evaluate the results. If I feel candidates are ducking the issue, or throwing in too much trivia, or trying to steer the conversation around a tricky point, then I will dive back in and take more control with progressively more direct and closed questions.

However, not everyone likes to operate in that style. If you prefer to feel in control of the conversation all of the time, then you will need to signal that to candidates early on. The chances are that interviewees will not be so forthcoming and you will need to keep up a constant flow of questions which help them to elaborate.

Note-taking
If you are doing a lot of interviews, then it is unlikely that you will be able to remember all the necessary details at the end of the day. So you will probably need to take some notes. However, do try to avoid appearing to be writing a major biography during the interview. The candidate will be justifiably curious and the flow of the conversation will be halted. Keep your notes to a few brief words which you write up after this interview but BEFORE the next.

Ending the interview
When you have covered all areas, bring the event to a close. You should make sure that the candidate has the opportunity to ask questions. Very often I also ask, 'Is there anything that you would like to have said that you haven't had a chance to say?' Having done all that, there is one very

important final point, the summary. At the end of the interview, summarize where you have got to and what will happen next. Say how you will contact the interviewee, and when. Also explain if you haven't already, what stage the selection process is at, e.g., 'We are seeing a number of people over the next five days and we will write to you one way or the other by the end of this month.' Check that things like expenses have been covered, and show the person out.

In a few cases, it becomes apparent that the candidate is not suitable for the job. If the reason is obvious and not negotiable, then it may be sensible to bring the interview to a close earlier than planned. The interview can have public relations benefits or drawbacks—one retail chain I know reminds all its managers that every interviewee is also a potential customer and can influence a lot of other potential customers. So if you are tempted to tell the candidate on the spot that they haven't got the job, please tread carefully.

An example—A selection interview

Mary Douglas, the data processing manager of a mail-order company in Birmingham, is interviewing Kevin Ronson, who has applied for a job as a systems analyst. Kevin is 28, has a degree in chemistry and has worked for three previous companies. He lives in Manchester. Mary has been seeing several candidates that morning and is running about fifteen minutes late. She has made sure that Kevin was told about the delay when he arrived, and given a cup of coffee and some material about the company to read while waiting. She has collected him from the waiting area.

MD: 'Come in Kevin, I'm sorry about the delay, would you like another cup of coffee? . . . Do you know Birmingham at all?'

Comment: This is purely an ice breaker, but it also signals that the interviewer is aware that she has kept the candidate waiting.

KR: 'No. I've only visited Birmingham once before and that was when I was a kid.'

Comment: If he is going to move to Birmingham, he will need to learn his way around.

MD: 'We've got about 45 minutes for this interview, and the way I'd like to play it is to start off by asking you some questions about yourself and your background, and your DP experience, and then to describe the job and discuss it with you. If you do have any questions about the job please do feel free to ask them then.'

Comment: Mary wants to control the interview fairly closely at first, so she tells Kevin how long she sees the interview taking and asks him to postpone any questions until later. She takes the risk that there is something that Kevin wants to ask early on which may affect the direction of the conversation but, in the circumstances, it is probably a reasonable risk.

MD: 'So let me start with your school work. Which of your three 'A' level subjects did you most enjoy, and what did you like about it?'

Comment: This should be a fairly easy question to start off with. Mary is aware that Kevin may be a bit nervous—especially because of the extra wait—and this kind of question should help him relax a little.

KR: 'I suppose maths was the best. I liked the teacher, but also I liked working on problems and solving them for myself.'

MD: 'What sort of problems?'

KR: 'Usually the sort that had a clear solution. I liked to get an equation to fall out into a clear pattern. What mathematicians would call an elegant solution.'

Comment: By staying with open questions, Mary is getting Kevin to elaborate on his subject. There may well be some more information to tie into this later on.

MD: 'So you went to Swansea to read chemistry. Had you any ideas of what sort of career this might lead to?'

KR: 'Not really. I assumed that it would be something in the scientific field. At that time I was most interested in physical chemistry and that was where I expected to specialize.'

Comment: Mary takes a chance that although she asks a closed question, it stimulates an open answer, and she is right. She has now unearthed two apparently conflicting statements. Perhaps it is time to confront a little. . .

MD: 'There's something I'm not quite clear on here. How was it that your favourite subject at school was maths, and yet you went to university to read chemistry?'

KR: 'Well yes, that was a bit funny. I got much better grades at chemistry than at maths, and I wanted to go to university, so my teachers advised me to apply for chemistry.'

MD: 'Why do you think your exam results were like that?'

KR: 'Well, probably because I tended to get too engrossed in a maths problem . . . looking for the best, or at least the most elegant solution really. It meant that I never finished any of the papers.'

Comment: In a relatively short time Mary has uncovered some potentially quite important information. How does Kevin tackle problems? Is he realistic at estimating how long it will take to come up with a solution? Does he get so engrossed that he loses touch with reality? If he knew this was a weakness, why didn't he do something about it? Did he listen to advice?

MD: 'Did anyone ever coach you in exam technique?'

KR: 'Oh yes, my teachers were always commenting on it, but I found some of the problems so interesting that I lost all track of time. And sometimes I did produce an original answer.'

Comment: So we have established that at school he didn't listen, but could produce high-quality work that could sometimes be out of the ordinary. At that stage he had difficulty in working to time. The question is, how does he do his work now? Mary will have to find this out during the next stage of the interview.

Mary has asked Kevin about his earlier jobs, and has now reached his present employer.

MD: 'You have explained why you were getting restless at your previous company, but what attracted you to Computabrain?'

KR: 'Partly it was the location. They had just moved to a Science Park on the outskirts of Manchester, and my wife's family come from near there, and we felt it would be nice to see more of them. But also Computabrain had just started using the new ICN 2470 sytem, and I felt that the opportunity to work with state-of-the-art equipment and systems would be interesting and improve my career prospects.'

MD: 'You saw the move to Computabrain as a short-term career move?'

Comment: Mary reflects back what Kevin has said, but has rephrased it without the gloss. She is checking out one possible meaning of what he said.

KR: 'Well, yes and no. I didn't go there thinking I'd only stay for a certain time, but neither did I expect to spend the rest of my life there. I felt that I would prefer at some point to leave that kind of software consultancy and move into a job where I would be working in a business for which the software was a support but not the business itself.'

Comment: He is being cautious, but also is saying that he likes working in an applied role. This could be some evidence that he has changed his style since school. Mary decides to leave this approach for the moment and gather a bit more data.

MD: 'Tell me about some of the projects that you have managed at Computabrain?'

KR: 'The biggest one I dealt with was where we were installing a system to manage the stock and inventory of one of our existing clients, a pharmaceutical company. There were about 5000 different items in all, and we had to design a system that would not only handle the normal requirements, but could also give a lot of extra detail on batch numbers, shelf life and expiry dates. It turned out to be quite a complex system in the end.'

MD: 'With that level of complexity, how did you plan to evaluate the effectiveness of the system?'

KR: 'Well, we set up a fairly detailed operating specification with the client, and we met all the requirements that had been asked for.'

Comment: Mary is after a bit more than that for an answer. On her person specification, she is interested in someone who is able to help clients to get a system that is useful, even if clients do not know precisely what they want. She has another go.

MD: 'Yes, I understand that, but sometimes the client doesn't know what to ask for. How did you make sure that he got the best possible system?'

KR: 'We had a working party, and we spent a lot of time talking about the system that they had working already and how we might need to change it in order to put it on our system. After a while we had enough data to be able to write a detailed specification. By that time the client was keen to buy our system as soon as we could provide it.'

Comment: The open question has produced some results, but there are still some ambiguities in what Kevin is saying.

MD: 'Why do you think your client was so keen to buy?'

KD: 'Partly because it was a good system. But also partly, I suppose, because there was an urgent need to replace the old methods.'

MD: 'Did your development time take longer than you originally thought?'

KD: 'Er, yes it did actually.'

MD: 'How much longer?'

KD: 'Er, well, it was all very difficult, because there was never just one client to talk to. Different people kept on appearing, and changing the requirements of the previous person. In the end we were running six months late and my director and the pharmaceutical director met and agreed a compromise specification.'

Comment: When pushed, Kevin reveals that the project wasn't so well managed, and the client probably did not get the best system. Of course this may not have been Kevin's fault, since the client may have continually moved the goalposts. However, it will be a useful way to find out how Kevin tackles the problem of helping clients to unravel what they really want.

We will move on to a later stage in the interview when Mary is asking Kevin about his ideas for the future.

MD: 'If you joined us you would be working directly with line managers and specialists. You would need to learn something about their jobs to be able to talk their language. How would you do that?'

KD: 'One of the reasons that I want to move out of my present software house is that I am working on so many projects with so many kinds of company that I never really get to know what any of them is about. I would very much like to spend some time with some of the managers that I would be providing and maintaining systems for. I think it is important for me to understand them and for them to understand me. So I would like to involve them in my work too.'

MD: 'We have talked about the kind of set-up we have here. If you joined us, what kinds of developments would you like to see us making?'

KD: 'I think you will need to upgrade both your hardware and the system. I would expect that over the next few years more of your staff will be looking for networking facilities, and that in itself will open up a whole range of possibilities.'

Comment: Mary was expecting to be told that the system needed upgrading, but she was pleased to hear a reference to the staff's needs. Both hypothetical questions have provided some supplementary data, but cannot be relied on too much since the candidate may be giving you what he feels you would like to hear rather than say he doesn't know. A version of one of the classic hypothetical questions is just coming up. . .

MD: 'So far you have changed jobs fairly regularly in order to progress your career. If you joined us, how would you see your career progressing over, say, the next five or ten years?'

KD: 'I think I would like to stay longer in a company now. I have moved up quite rapidly, but now I want to broaden my own range as a manager. I don't see myself staying as a systems analyst for ever and I would like to develop towards more general management. I'm going to stand a much better chance of doing that by staying with one company.'

Comment: It may all be rubbish, but it sounds like well thought out rubbish—which is all you can ask for from that sort of question.

Mary asks Kevin if he has any questions, deals with those, and then summarizes.

MD: 'I am interviewing a number of people over the next two weeks to choose a shortlist to come back and meet the managing director. So I will not be able to write to you for at least a fortnight. If we do call you back it will be for a half a day so that you could meet a number of people.

Thank you for coming, and would you let my secretary have details of your expenses on your way out.'

Comment: It is always worth while letting candidates know what happens next, especially if there will be some delay before a decision is made.

The selection interview: summary checklist
1. Draw up a plan.
2. Areas to cover:
    School/job history
    Outside activities
    Hypothetical examples
3. Circumstances:
    No interruptions
    Clear desk
    Room layout
    Coffee, smoking and other personal comforts
    Timing
4. The interview:
    Explain the purpose
    Use open questions at first, closed later
    Use a style and level of control that is comfortable
    Keep note-taking brief
    Finish with a summary.

4
The appraisal interview

The idea of appraisal is widespread among commercial and other organizations. However, the purpose of the appraisal can be enormously varied. Different managers and different organizations use the same word and yet with quite different meanings. With all of the interviews in this book, I have tried to stress the importance of knowing why you are conducting that interview. With appraisals, this is especially important.

Purpose

If your organization has an appraisal system, then someone somewhere has thought through why the system is used. If you are not clear, then it's worth checking, since it would be a pity to be out of step with the rest of the organization.

In companies I have worked with, I have come across at least nine quoted reasons for doing appraisals:
1. To review performance (often over the last year).
2. To find ways of improving subordinate (and boss?) performance.
3. To correct poor performance.
4. To plan and set future objectives.
5. To assess potential for development and promotion.
6. To assess salary, merit, or bonus.
7. To discuss current operating problems.
8. To provide data for the company succession and manpower plan.
9. To keep the personnel department quiet.

It must be said that many organizations expect their appraisal systems to meet several of the aims quoted above. This is fine, except that some of them will be in conflict.

Salary v. *performance improvement*

If you and I were to sit down and talk about how you could improve your performance, then one of the assumptions underlying our discussion would be that there was room for improvement. In the words of the eternal school report, 'could do better'. A detailed discussion of how you could do better will look at occasions when you made mistakes, took poor decisions, and generally weren't at your best. Calmly and rationally, we examine the problems that you faced at the time, and work through how you might tackle a similar situation if it arose in future. For this process to work effectively, you have to feel comfortable about 'admitting' your errors. Otherwise how can you learn from them? The whole discussion has to be carried out in an atmosphere which does not punish you for admitting doing something badly.

So what's wrong with that, you may be saying. The problem comes if you try to incorporate something like a salary or bonus review into the same discussion. If our organization links pay to performance and you and I were discussing your salary, then you are likely to want to go for everything you can get. Over the years a lot of people have told me that they are underpaid, while very very few have said that they were overpaid. If we are discussing pay, then to some extent we are negotiating. If we are negotiating, then I suspect that you are far less likely to 'admit' to doing anything badly, since you know it will affect your pay. You will find yourself edging towards the argument that you couldn't have performed better at the time, and so your salary should not suffer. The assumption that there is always room for improvement, and that improvement is possible, has more or less gone by the board.

What can be done? A lot of organizations separate their salary reviews from their appraisals. On an annual system, you can separate them by up to six months. If that is not possible, then the next best thing is to make some kind of distinction between the performance review meeting and the salary review meeting. In a company that relates pay to performance, it is inevitable that people will make some links between how their appraisal went and how their pay was adjusted. However, when people know that they can improve their pay by improving their performance, it may just help them to accept that they can improve.

Performance v. *potential*

Many appraisals expect to look at recent performance and also review potential for the future. This mix seems to work quite well, but there are some traps. The first is that a person's performance in the current job may not be a very good predictor of how they would do in some future job: the good sales rep may be a poor sales manager. If you are expected to assess potential, then you may need to ask some hypothetical questions. It would also be worth while distinguishing between the parts of the person's job which might become more important if they were promoted and the parts that they would be expected to give up.

The second trap is to imply that the person is being offered promotion. It is quite easy for a slip of the tongue to give the impression that it is only a matter of time before promotion takes place. A discussion on future potential needs to set the ground rules carefully. If you are asking the person where they see their career going, and what you see as their potential, then you must make sure that you don't appear to make promises that you cannot keep.

The third trap that exists is to let the person think that their personal development and career development are something that the organization alone can look after. Very few organizations have a guaranteed escalator of career development for even their fast-track staff. In any discussion of the future it is important that individuals recognize that they have at least as much responsibility for their own development as the organization that employs them.

Personnel v. *line management*
Unfortunately, in many organizations it is felt that the appraisal system is operated mainly for the benefit of the personnel department. Here is a quote from a line manager:

> Personnel sends out the forms once a year and then nags us until we get the ***** things back to them. We don't see any results and, as far as we know, the forms stay in a personnel filing cabinet. Can you blame us if we get them out of the way as fast as possible?

If the appraisal system is regarded in this way, then it is hardly surprising that managers don't take all that much care in getting the system to work properly. If, on the other hand, line managers see the appraisal as something which will help them to do their job better, then the whole system can work very effectively. Personnel departments stand to gain a lot of useful information from an effective appraisal scheme, and so it is in their interest to make sure that line managers recognize it as a management technique rather than a personnel imposition.

The system that you are working with will very often be based around an appraisal form. The form, or copies of it, will probably have to be sent to the personnel department. If you don't know what they do with it, now is the time to find out, BEFORE you fill the thing in. Anyway, your appraisee might ask you, and it would be foolish not to know. Whatever the final destination of the form, don't forget that the conversation can cover a much wider ground than the form reports. Even if the system does belong to the personnel department, you can still make it work to your advantage as long as you construct your interview to meet both personnel's and your own needs.

Preparation
Rather obviously, the preparation you do will depend on what you perceive the purpose of the event to be. Let us assume that your appraisal is to cover a review of the past year and some discussion about future prospects. What kinds of preparation can you do?

Collect information
Your preparation for the appraisal can start almost a year before the interview actually takes place. To be able to review all aspects of someone's performance it is important that you have kept a note of the work that has been done over the year. It is no good just talking about what has happened in the last few weeks. A comprehensive summary is the only thing that will do both of you justice.

Keep a note of incidents that have happened and tasks that have been performed—good and bad—to jog your memory when you are discussing performance. If you are going to criticize someone's performance, then you will need to have sufficient evidence to present to the person to be able to convince them to change their ways. In the same way, it is important to be able to praise the things that have gone well. Specific praise works much better than a general 'looks fine to me'.

Of course, keeping a note of incidents and the like is no substitute for dealing with problems at the time. The appraisal is not the moment to bring new information out into the open. It is to be hoped that none of the discussion on performance will cover new ground; but it will be an opportunity to take a wide perspective on how the person works—what goes well and what doesn't.

Appraisee's preparation
For the interview to go well, both the appraiser and the appraisee should have done some preparation. You need to give the appraisee some notice of the interview, and some idea of the structure that will be used. Some

appraisal systems include an appraisee preparation form. Some managers give appraisees a copy of the appraisal form and ask them to fill it in for themselves. If appraisees have not had the time to prepare, because you have sprung it on them, then you cannot expect a very constructive discussion. Appraisees should also be encouraged to think about their current and future training needs and, if appropriate, their future career development.

In a few appraisal systems, appraisees are asked to comment on what their boss could do to improve their joint effectiveness. What could the boss do to improve performance? To handle this part of the meeting, the appraisee should have done the same as the boss, and collected some data relating to the points to be made.

In many ways appraisees' preparation methods will be quite similar to those of their boss. Appraisees may want to put their point of view and discuss why they thought they performed effectively or not. If the discussion can focus on specific incidents rather than generalized opinions, then there is a much better chance that performance can be improved.

Performance standards
Part of the review of performance will look at the standards of performance that were set. Did the appraisee reach the standards set? Were the standards realistic? What could be done next year to reach higher standards, or to be more certain of reaching those that are set?

At some stage during the interview, performance standards and targets may be set for the following year. These need to be compared with previous targets and possible problem areas anticipated. Performance standards fall into two kinds. They may be numeric, i.e., a number of sales calls made per day, scrap rate down to x per cent. Or they may be describable only in words and by comparison, i.e., 'you should look smart and well groomed whenever meeting potential customers; you should make yourself more available to supervisors on the shop floor—follow Jim's example.'

The interview
You need to structure the interview so as to cover all the points on the appraisal form. Many people tend to use the form as a guide to the format they should use. However, there is no need to slavishly follow the form. The conversation can be wider ranging, if this is going to be useful to you and the appraisee.

It is important to allow yourself enough time, and to try and hold off interruptions. No one is likely to want to discuss their future career development in an office that seems more like an airline terminal. That said, it is sometimes better to get away from the office altogether. It may buy you more time, fewer disturbances and perhaps a bit more relaxation. But if you choose the pub, do remember that it is a business meeting, not a night out! Also, if you are in the local, how do you deal with bumping into someone that you know?

The content of the interview is going to depend on the data that you have already collected. Most of that work should have been done already—your job in the interview is to bring it all together to make sense to the appraisee. You will probably have some aspects of the work that you wish to praise, you will probably also have some aspects which you feel could be improved on for the following year. Training needs and career prospects may also be on the agenda.

Structure of the interview

A good place to start is with a review of the past year. Go through the various things that have happened—good and bad—and pick out the events that you wish to talk about. A useful technique is to ask appraisees how they thought they did on a particular piece of work. Getting their view first allows you to structure your comment to try to build on what has been said. You will want to give your opinion, but if it is critical, remember that most people have learned from their schooldays how to brush off criticism. You want to create an atmosphere of problem-solving rather than staff-bashing, so temper your comments so that appraisees can learn from them. After all, if you do not believe that they can do better, why are you wasting time with this appraisal? You should be going straight for a disciplinary interview instead.

The appraisee will probably want to raise some matters about the events you have highlighted. You can discuss your different points of view and if possible resolve your differences. What you are always doing is talking about specific examples of what happened. You can praise things that went well, and discuss ways of preventing a recurrence of things that went badly: all the time you have real examples to use as evidence of what is wanted next time. Appraisals go wrong because people talk in generalities, and are not able or willing to give specific examples of what they mean. The result is that neither side has communicated effectively, and neither gets what they want.

Quite possibly the bulk of the time will be spent on this analysis of the past year's work and the lessons to be learned from it. At some stage you will want to move on to talk about the future. You may have some concrete plans for the appraisee or for the business, or it may just be kite-flying. Be clear what it is you are discussing. An imaginative appraisee may believe that you are actually offering that new branch manager-ship—whereas you were only 'sounding him out'. Use hypothetical questions if you wish but, again, remember that the bush telegraph will have told your appraisee what is likely and possible.

The other aspect of discussions about the future is that assumptions are often made about the line of work that an appraisee wants to stay in. It may just be that you have someone sitting before you who wants to make a career change. Don't angle all your questions to assume that 'once an accountant always an accountant'. It is hackneyed to say it, but people do change. Their work and domestic needs change, and just because they have done similar work, or been in the same industry for umpteen years, doesn't mean you can assume that they will always want to stay there. Obviously not everyone is or wants to be a Paul Gauguin, but the appraisal that doesn't offer the opportunity to let the appraisee talk may miss some real potential which could benefit the organization.

Training needs are often discussed at appraisals. The classic negative line goes something like: 'Well what training courses do you want to go on?', to which the classic reply is; 'I don't know because you never send me on anything I ask for anyway.' In my view, training needs should not be left to the end of the discussion and thrown in as an afterthought, or because there is a box for it on the form. If someone needs to be trained it is because there is an opportunity for them to perform better or do different work. Real training needs should emerge as part of the discussion on past performance and how to improve it, or as a result of plans for future work.

Style

While appraisal interviews can be conducted effectively in a variety of styles, it has to be said that anything too formal is going to sound more like a disciplinary than an appraisal interview. If your style is to tell people what they've done wrong and order them to pull their socks up, then do not be surprised if your best people leave, and the others don't actually know what it is they have to do better. If you really want them to improve their performance, then they are likely to do much better with a mixture of praise and criticism which they can act on. A more relaxed, informal style will serve you far better, especially if this idea of joint problem-solving can be set up.

It follows, from what has just been said, that an effective discussion will allow both appraiser and appraisee to have some control over the exact structure of the meeting. If, as the appraiser, you can steer the general direction of the discussion without getting too worried about losing control, then appraisees will feel that they have had a reasonable chance to put their views forward and be listened to. From the appraisees' perspective, to go to the meeting with ideas and points to make and then not be allowed to make them, is very frustrating, and demotivating too. So, as the appraiser, be prepared to listen.

It would also help if you weren't always right. Or at least, if something has gone wrong, if you are prepared to admit that you made a mistake as well. Of course the caricature of the boss is that he (it's always he!) is all knowing, all powerful, and always right. In the real world, we know that our bosses are only human and that inevitably they make mistakes, just like the rest of us. So as a boss, why don't you admit to being human? Your staff will respect you more for it, and if you can both learn how to avoid making that mistake in future, then you have improved overall performance. It is at this stage that many appraisals become joint problem-solving meetings.

Joint problem-solving

If both appraisee and appraiser accept that they can improve their performance, then the appraisal is a good opportunity for both to learn how to improve. Regarding the appraisal in this way is only likely to work if there is sufficient trust between both participants. If this is the case, then the appraisal can be immensely useful.

The joint problem-solving approach requires both parties to focus on the problems and the behaviour needed to solve those problems. Once you feel you have a solution to the problem, then you will need to draw up an action plan. You do this in your summary.

Summary and action plan

Whatever it is that you have agreed during the interview, always make time at the end to summarize and agree an action plan. Ideally the plan should have review dates and criteria against which success can be measured. It need not take long, it should be written down, and a copy kept by each participant. Then it is easy to do some following up.

Follow-up

The only true measure of effectiveness for an appraisal interview is whether anything happens as a result of it. If you have been discussing improved performance, then you must follow up to see if performance really does improve. Use the summary and action plan, and check up what has happened: it is a good discipline for you and the appraisee. It will also help performance, since your original plan may not have been perfect and may need some modifications if it is to work well.

An example—An appraisal interview

Ann Thomas is the first branch manager of a fairly recently opened branch of a building society. The Archway and Marble building societies merged about two years previously, and opened a number of new branches under the new name of the Marble Arch building society. Ann has spent most of her career with Archway. Her assistant branch manager, Sandra Plant, has spent most of her career with Marble.

The appraisal interview is taking place slightly less than a year after the branch opened. They are using the Archway appraisal scheme which includes a form for the appraisee to complete. Ann gave Sandra about two weeks' notice that the appraisal was to take place, and provided her with a description of the system and a copy of the form that Ann would fill in and that they would both have to sign. Ann has chosen a time when there are usually few interruptions, and has arranged cover for all normal enquiries that might come to either of them. The conversation has started, and they are just beginning the review of the previous year.

AT: 'It's been a very full year for all of us, Sandra. For you, what have been the highlights and the lowlights?'

Comment: Ann asks a wide open question to involve Sandra and get her views right from the start.

SP: 'Well, I think we've all been very busy getting the branch really operational. I think I'm most pleased about us beating our target figures for new business. I suppose the frequent computer breakdowns were the most disappointing.'

Comment: Ann wants to discuss several aspects of Sandra's performance, and these points are two of them. If possible Ann will try to get Sandra to recognize for herself areas that she could improve upon.

AT: 'Well, first of all, let me say that everyone is very pleased with the extra business that has been brought in. I know that you have personally worked very hard to get the branch off to a flying start. I showed you the reports from the regional manager and I know he is very pleased about the level of business. But I am worried that you are putting in too many hours. (With a smile) Is there a danger that you are becoming indispensable?'

SP: 'I know I did put in a lot of time, but there seemed to be so many things to be done. And with us having taken on several new staff who were untrained, it was a lot faster and more accurate if I did things myself rather than let them do it and then have to correct it afterwards.'

Comment: This is one of the points that Ann wants to raise with Sandra. She is very reluctant to delegate, and her career development depends on her being able to show that she can manage staff, not just be good at the work they do. Also, when Ann praised her, she praised the level of business. She did not make some kind of blanket statement implying that ALL was well, because not all of it is. It would be a contradiction to later talk about some of the problems.

AT: 'Everyone is very impressed with the commitment you have shown this past year, and the way you have tackled all sorts of work to keep the branch going. But stepping back from the day-to-day work, and bearing in mind that it is always easier to "do it yourself" rather than training someone else to: how well do you think you have allocated your time, especially during, say, the last three months?'

Comment: Ann is trying to get Sandra to see that she has got into a fixed pattern of automatically taking some of the harder work from the other clerical staff in the branch. Ann suspects she got into this pattern during the early months when many of the staff were new. But now they should be doing much more of the work.

SP: 'Er, that's a hard one. I suppose that I've just tried to keep the workload down, and not to let any backlogs build up too high. Are you saying that I could have done more? Surely you aren't saying that I could have worked any harder?'

AT: 'Certainly not. But I am concerned that you see the workload as your personal responsibility. And sometimes that means you feel you have to deal with it personally rather than letting the other clerical staff deal with more of it.'

Comment: Ann has to tread very carefully here. She does not want to discourage Sandra from all her enthusiasm for making the branch successful. On the other hand, Sandra needs to delegate more and in doing so allow the other branch staff to develop their own skills.

SP: 'But you know that many of the staff are new. If I gave some of the harder work to them, there would almost certainly be mistakes which I would have to catch and correct. Regional Office is not going to stay pleased with us if we let through mortgages at the wrong rates.'

AT: 'Of course we need to maintain our accuracy, but mortgage agreements have to be countersigned by you or me anyway, and then the computer cross-checks the whole thing afterwards. When was the last time that one of the other staff sat down with a customer and took them through a mortgage agreement?'

Comment: In order to make her point, Ann will have to be specific, and quote Sandra examples of work she could have delegated.

SP: 'Well, actually, I don't think that anyone ever has. I've always felt it was too important to let anyone else do it.'

AT: 'When you were a clerk, how did you learn to handle mortgage enquiries?'

Comments: The thought that what works for you might also work for others is a simple but powerful argument.

SP: 'The assistant branch manager showed me, and then sat with me while I did a couple. . . . OK, I see the point. If I don't do the same, then my staff will not be able to learn either. But I still feel that it is taking a risk.'

AT: 'At first, just let them sit in and watch you. Then swap over and you sit in and watch them. Only when you are both reasonably happy do you pull out and let them go solo. Even then, I should make a point of glancing through the paperwork before it is finally sent off.'

Comment: Ann has made some progress, but she still needs to agree an action plan.

AT: 'If you agree, I'd like to agree a programme of planned delegation with you. How could we do that?'

SP: 'I could draw up a list of the tasks in the branch that I currently do and mark the ones that I think could be delegated. But I think I'd want some help in deciding who to delegate to, and how to hand over the work without too much risk.'

Comment: Ann is not telling Sandra what to do. She is agreeing with Sandra a plan that they will both feel committed to.

AT: 'Of course I'll be pleased to help. If you could do your list fairly soon then we can arrange to meet and discuss it early next week.'

(They agree a date)

AT: 'Once we can get you delegating more I think that there will be two benefits. The first will be to train other members of branch staff in a wider range of the work we do. The second, which I see as just as important, will be to free up some of your time. I'd prefer it if you didn't have to work such long hours, but also I'd like to involve you in more of what I've been doing over the last few months. What do you think about that?''

SP: 'I'd like that. I have concentrated on being good as an assistant branch manager, so I haven't really thought much further ahead.'

AT: 'Well, in the same way that I am urging you to help the more junior branch staff develop, the same reasoning applies to me. What would you see as your next main career move?'

Comment: As the opportunity has arisen to look into the future, Ann is taking it.

SP: 'I think that I'd like to spend a little time in Head Office before coming back to branch management. I don't really know what goes on up there, but I feel it would be important to at least have a few contacts. It would help when the computers failed.'

AT: 'Do you know much about the computer system?'

SP: 'No, not really. Why?'

AT: 'Well, a good way for you to learn about Head Office is to go up there a few times. How would you feel about that?'

SP: 'I would like that.'

AT: 'A very good reason to go would be to increase your knowledge of the present and planned computer systems, and how they fit into branch management. That way you would meet some people and get yourself known a bit. You might even discover how to make the wretched things more reliable. Do you think you could manage that?'

SP: 'I think that would be very good, but I doubt that I'll bring back a magic wand.'

Comment: Ann has found a way for Sandra to improve her performance on her present job by increasing her knowledge. But in doing so, she is also improving her longer-term career development prospects.

(The conversation continues over a number of other topics. At the end Ann makes a complete summary, and shows Sandra what she is going to write on the appraisal form. Sandra signs the form to say that it is an accurate record of the conversation.)

The appraisal interview: summary checklist
1. Clarify the *purpose* before you start:
    (a) Performance review
        Improvements needed
        Successes recognized
    Potential assessment
        Making the best use of appraisee's abilities
        Developing the appraisee
    (b) Salary review
2. Preparation:
    Give appraisee some notice
    Review performance standards
    Gather specific examples
3. The interview:
    Use real examples, i.e., from past year's performance
    Let appraisee speak
    Adopt a problem-solving approach
    Summarize and agree an action plan at the end
4. Follow up the action plan to ensure it is implemented.

5
The counselling interview

The counselling interview is different from all the others in this book, for two reasons. The first is that there is often very little specific preparation that the interviewer can do prior to the first interview, usually for the simple reason that what the interviewee wants to say is private and should not be divulged to anyone in advance of the meeting. The second is that this is the one kind of interview where the interviewer may wish to give control over to the interviewee for quite long periods of time.

Whose problem is it anyway?
However, the starting-off point for most interviewers is that somebody wants to see them and won't say what it's about. Often the opening phase is confused and even camouflaged with some other subject. Every doctor has heard something along the lines of: 'Doctor, doctor I have a close friend who has this personal problem. . ' People turn up in your office to talk about something and then, just as they are going, they say, 'Oh, by the way, there was something I'd like your opinion on. . . ', or people bump into you with 'Have you got a moment?' Whatever it is, they are likely to be looking for three things:

● Someone to listen to them
● Advice
● Direct assistance.

Your problem as the interviewer is that you don't know what the problem is about, and at the early stage of the discussion you may not know whose problem it is at all. The professional counsellor is always at pains to establish very early on just who is the client. It may be that the person you are talking to is acting as a go-between and is only indirectly involved in the problem. It may be that you are being asked to take sides in some disagreement between two people who are both trying to get you on their side. Whatever it is, and however complicated, it is essential that you understand who you are trying to help and why.

If you are able to make some preparations, then try to find a quiet spot in which the conversation can take place without interruptions. A person is hardly likely to want to speak freely when surrounded by ringing telephones and people popping in to ask a quick question. As you will not be controlling the greater part of the interview, you cannot predict how long it will take. It is safer to err on the generous side, and allow plenty of time before your next appointment. If you know, or suspect, what the problem might be then you can do some preliminary work by sounding out other people, checking on company policy and rules if relevant, or discussing with your own boss what possible solutions exist.

The first stage of the interview
At the first meeting, the interviewee may take some time to get to the point and may need to be helped but not rushed. It may be that the first stage is just to establish that you are prepared to try to help and to do that in a confidential and private environment. Bear in mind that the interviewee may have been worrying about this for months before bringing it to you, even though this may well be the first that you have heard of it. Don't be surprised therefore, it there is a dreadful tangle of emotion, fact, opinion and logic. Most of us have had the experience of something going round and round in our heads until we are almost desperate to tell someone about it: this may be what has happened to your interviewee.

Deal with the emotion first
The professional counsellor will frequently have to deal with an emotional client, and knows very well that while the interviewee is in an emotional state it will be very hard for them to discuss how to solve the problem logically. If you find yourself confronted by someone who is angry, or in tears, or emotional in any way, the first thing to do is to deal with the emotion.

You have two options. The first is to do nothing and just be with the person. The second is to do something, and that usually means talking about whatever the problem is. Someone who has suffered a great shock may not want people to talk to them or give them cups of tea or whatever, but may just want someone to be there. People in a state of emotional shock are frequently unaware of time. It may seem to go slower or faster, but it will not be the same for them as for you. So bear this in mind when helping them to cope with the emotion first.

Someone who is angry will often perceive your responses in a distorted way: whatever you say is likely to be misunderstood. You will therefore need to communicate very clearly. For instance, anything that you say or do that can be interpreted as threatening will probably prolong the anger, and delay the opportunity to do something constructive about the problem.

A plan for effective counselling
A counselling interview is often the least structured of the kinds of interviews that a manager has to do. However, there are three recognizable stages which you will go through in order to reach a conclusion that meets the needs of the interviewee.

- Establishing trust
- Identifying and exploring the problem
- Helping the interviewee reach a solution.

Let us look at each of these in order.

Establishing trust
Most of the counselling that you do will be with people that you know. Even so, interviewees may still need reassurance that you are prepared to listen. They will often want specific evidence that you are to be trusted in these particular circumstances, even though under normal circumstances they know you and work with you. There are a number of ways that you can build up trust between yourself and the interviewee.

1. Your stance and posture will be giving signals to the interviewee which will indicate if you are relaxed and interested in what you are being told. A lack of eye-contact, tension in your face, surreptitious glances at your watch, will signal that you wish you could get this interview over as fast as possible so that you can get down to some useful work. In that case although the interviewee may go away, it is unlikely that the problem will. In fact it will probably get worse!
2. If the story that an interviewee is telling you is confused and difficult to follow, it is important that you help unravel the strands as you go along. A process called active listening can be helpful. What you do is to make brief summaries of what you think the interviewee has

said at pauses during the conversation. Doing this helps in two ways. First, it helps the interviewee know that you are listening and paying attention. (Think how irritating it is to hear only silence when speaking to someone on the telephone. Most people like to get quite frequent feedback confirming that the listener is still there.) Second, it makes sure that what you thought the interviewee said is actually what was meant. It means that all the way through the interview you are checking your understanding of the message the interviewee is sending. As a by-product it may help the interviewee to clarify their own muddled ideas. But the time for that tends to be in the second stage of the interview.

3. If the subject matter of the interviewee's problem is confidential, painful or perhaps embarrassing, then the counsellor may have to prove their sensitivity to the potential of the subject. Some interviewees will talk about their problems once they have received an assurance of confidentiality. However, other interviewees seem to need a more concrete demonstration of this. Here the counsellor may find it useful to talk about personal experiences, especially if they have been similar to the ones described by the interviewee. If you can talk honestly and openly about your emotions at that time you will help the interviewee to cope with their own emotions now. You will also be demonstrating that you are prepared to trust the interviewee with some information about yourself, and therefore why shouldn't the interviewee trust you?

As an aside to this, I remember reading the memoirs of a famous Fleet Street gossip columnist. He said that the reason he was able to find out so much about the rich and famous was because he was prepared to tell them about his own troubles. They then seemed to feel honour bound to match one of his stories with one of their own. As he claimed to have led a considerably less than perfect existence, he had lots of material to work with. This doesn't mean that the good counsellor will have had a go at every possible wrong and problem that humans have devised! Nor is it an opportunity to regale everyone you come across with all the bad times you have had—especially if it comes out in some kind of competitive 'I've had more problems than you have' sort of style. But it does mean that the person with no common links with the interviewee is going to find it hard to establish credibility and empathy.

Identifying and exploring the problem
Doctors often find that the problem the patient brings to them is not the

real problem at all. A patient will raise some other matter on leaving the surgery, and that is the really worrying one. I have heard it said that if doctors could have the last 30 seconds of each consulting interview first, then they could be of much more help to their patients.

When a person first comes to see you they will be bringing a mixture of:

- Symptoms
- Causes
- Solutions.

In this stage of the interview your role is to help the interviewee to unscramble the mixture and sort out what are causes and what are symptoms. Only at that stage can you go on to look at possible solutions.

Clarify, probe and reflect back
It may be that the interviewee has been made redundant, or has a personal problem, or needs advice on career direction. The problem may appear clear cut to the interviewee or it may appear very confused. Your job at this stage is to listen carefully to the words the interviewee is using and also to the non-verbal messages that are being sent. You will have to teach the interviewee to distinguish between symptoms, causes and solutions.

You will also need to ask questions and probe behind the thoughts that the interviewee is presenting to you. People often get locked into a particular thought pattern and start to believe that there really is only one way of looking at the problem. You can help the interviewee to explore alternatives and start to pave the way for finding solutions. On occasion it may be necessary to confront the interviewee with some unpalatable fact or proposition which may be contributing to the problem. It is easy to confront: a good mud-slinging row is knee-deep in confrontation. That type of confrontation seldom gets either party anywhere. What I am describing is helping the interviewee to first accept and then do something about a less attractive side of their behaviour. To do this effectively takes some skill, and cannot be attempted until a large amount of trust is established. Comments of the kind: 'you'd better pull yourself together and stop behaving like an idiot', are unlikely to produce results. However, a specific description of the behaviour and its effects will give the interviewee something to work on, such as: 'One reason why people ignore you may be that you tend to speak slowly and quietly, and usually only when you are spoken to. It would help if you could turn up your internal volume control a bit.'

Helping the interviewee reach a solution
The interviewee may open the interview with a statement about a solution. 'I need to go on a training course.' 'I need more time.' 'If only people would stay off my back.' Until you have helped them to explore and probe the problem, it is probably best to put ideas of how to solve it to one side, until you are both sure that you have covered the whole area. Then, at this final stage of the interview, start to look for appropriate solutions. Appropriate means a solution that the interviewee feels can be implemented successfully. There will probably be a great temptation for the interviewer to suggest—even impose—their own solution. This would be fine if the interviewer were the one with the problem; but of course the interviewer's real job is to help find a solution that is right for the interviewee.

The solution may come in several stages. It may not be possible for someone who has become overdependent on drink to suddenly just give it up and suffer no withdrawal effects. The process will have to be a gradual one. In the case of the alcoholic, it should certainly involve reference to professionals working in that field. Managers faced with a potentially alcoholic member of staff should not feel they could 'have a go at sorting the bloke out', but perhaps they could help the man to summon up the courage to admit that he has a problem for which qualified help is available. In itself that may be a major step.

Someone came to you originally for advice and possibly for direct assistance. There are two traps here for the willing but unwary helper. First, that the interviewee will come to depend in some way on the interviewer to solve all problems. Although there may be a number of things that you as a manager can do, please check that you are not taking over the problem from the interviewee, if it really is the interviewee's problem. The danger is that by taking on too much yourself you encourage the interviewee to regard you as the local problem-solving service, whereas you should be educating the interviewee to avoid these problems, or at least cope better in future. The second trap is tht the interviewee will knock down all the suggestions and ideas that the manager puts forward. It almost becomes a game, where the manager puts forward a proposal and the interviewee has to find a way of shooting it down. The interviewee is becoming dependent on the counsellor in a different way, and by finding objections to each idea is prolonging the counselling, and, of course, avoiding doing anything about the problem. In this kind of case, the counsellor may need to confront the interviewee with their avoidance behaviour, and help them to overcome that first.

Follow-up

Whatever your level of involvement in the interviewee's problem, it is most important to follow up what happens next. By agreeing to counsel the interviewee, you are taking on not just that particular set of problems, but also the task of training the interviewee to anticipate those problems in future. As a result of your counselling, the interviewee should have been set on a learning curve and it is essential that you keep track of progress. Teaching people to swim by throwing them in the swimming pool and walking away does nothing for either their swimming ability or their confidence.

An example—A redundancy counselling interview

Tony Walsh is the company secretary of an organization that has recently had to make a number of staff redundant. As company secretary, Tony is responsible for all personnel matters. Andy Sampson is one of those who have been made redundant. He has been with the company for 11 years and has worked his way up to be the most senior non-qualified member of the accounts department. He is 43, married and has two teenage children. Andy already knows of his redundancy, but now wants to ask Tony for help.

TW: 'I appreciate that this is a very hard time for you and your family, and that although rumours of redundancies have been flying around for some time, the news of your own redundancy must still have come as a shock. You've asked to see me, so perhaps you could start off.'

Comment: Tony expresses empathy with Andy (it's important that his manner, voice tone and facial expression support his words) and tries to build a bridge with his guess as to how Andy is feeling. He mentions the redundancy and also Andy's family, since he wants to show that he appreciates that the news will have hit them as hard as it has hit Andy. When people have had a shock, they often try to deny what has occurred. By using this opening, Tony is encouraging Andy to accept reality.

AS: 'Well, I think you've got a nerve sitting behind that desk in your secure job as the company secretary. It's alright for you to appreciate this or that, but you're not the one losing a job. Eleven years I've worked hard for this company, a lot longer than you've been here, and what thanks do I get . . . you seem to have sat around and invented a few rules and get your name on the company notepaper and you're keeping your job. Of course you've always kept in well with the managing director. . . .'

TW: (after Andy has run out of steam) 'Andy, I realize how strongly you feel, and I can understand that you feel angry with me and probably with most of the company. But did you come here just to tell me that or was there something else that you wanted to talk about?'

Comment: Andy is hurt and angry. He wants to hit out at something or someone, and it doesn't seem to matter who. Tony reflects the content of the message and the feelings associated with it but stays calm. He does not rise to the bait, and he does not let the various accusations that Andy is throwing around distract him from the real (and as yet unstated) purpose of the meeting. He reminds Andy of this with his last statement, in which he is careful not to fight back or condemn Andy for all the unfair things he is alleging.

AS: (after a bit more invective) 'Well, I also wanted to know about my redundancy money, and what I have to do after that. I mean, what do I tell them at the Job Centre, I suppose I shall have to go down there. And then there's my pension, and the mortgage and getting myself fixed up with another job. And anyway I'm 43 so I suppose most companies won't want to look at me; it's all computers nowadays and what can I offer, don't even know where to start. . . .'

Comment: Now we are beginning to get closer to what Andy really has on his mind. Of course the way he presents the information is confused, because Andy is confused. The first thing to do is to try and make some sense of the various strands.

TW: 'You have raised a number of points, Andy. The redundancy money and registering with the Job Centre are the easiest to deal with, so let's deal with those now . . . (Tony takes Andy through the mechanics of his redundancy payment and how to register at the Job Centre).—But as I understand you, your main concern is how to get yourself another job. Is that right?'

Comment: If there are matters that can be cleared out of the way immediately, then you might as well do so. It will demonstrate to the interviewee that at least some of his problems can be solved easily, and that in itself may give him more confidence. Tony also checks his understanding about what Andy sees as the main problem even though he is tempted to 'assume' it is obvious. Even with apparently obvious problems it is worth checking, since what is obvious to you may be nothing of the kind to the interviewee.

AS: 'Well of course it is, I don't think many companies are interested in a middle-aged accounts clerk.'

TW: 'Lets look at some of the options open to you. For instance, when was the last time you tested yourself out on the market?'

AS: 'What do you mean?'

TW: 'When did you last attend a job interview with an outside company?'

AS: 'Not for eleven years.'

TW: 'So you are somewhat rusty at the business of presenting yourself for interview, and being interviewed? That's one point to put on the action plan.'

AS: 'That's all very well, but how do I get to the interview in the first place? There are a lot of unemployed people around, you know. What can I say that I can do? I know our company's system, but that's not much use to anyone else.'

Comment: Tony is trying to move Andy towards an understanding of what he can do now, and what he will have to learn to do if he is to find himself another job. He has mentioned an action plan, and although Andy has argued back, he has not rejected the idea out of hand. Tony will now try to help Andy to think through some of the points for his action plan himself.

TW: 'Well, let's start at the beginning and look at what you could offer an organization. What do you think you are good at? Let us draw up a list of everything that you can do that might possibly be of interest to another company. Then we can start to work out a plan to make sure that the right company hears about you. (They work on that for a time.) Good, so now we have a list of the things that you can do already, but let's go broader than that. What do you think you could learn to do? And add to that what you think you would most like to do.'

Comment: The joint problem-solving approach means that Tony will have to ask most of the questions to start with, but gradually will encourage Andy to ask more questions for himself. Tony is careful to get Andy to provide the answers, although if he seems to have missed something obvious he can chip in his ideas too. But at no stage does Tony take over the problem.

TW: (They have now produced a lot of lists, and are sitting side by side at a table.) 'Can we review where we have got to? As I see it, you have quite a lot of strengths which are potentially saleable, and you have also identified which of those strengths you would be able to develop if necessary. What you now need to do is to write up a good curriculum vitae for yourself which you could send to some companies. Preparing that will also force you to think how to fill in job application forms—like the one the Job Centre will give you. You'll need to do some research in the newspapers for job adverts and also get your name down with all the agencies. You've got a lot of writing ahead of you, and if you could get at least some of it typed it would help make a good impression. I can't help you with all your correspondence, but I can willingly make sure that your cv is well typed and duplicated on our copier. I suggest that you go and discuss all these things with your wife. For instance, would you both be prepared to move to get a job? How much drop in salary could you accept? Would you be prepared to do contract work away from home? . . . . Then come back to see me in one week's time. We can review your draft cv and discuss how your job-hunting campaign is going.'

Comment: In any counselling interview, a summary should be linked with some kind of action plan, preferably tied to some dates or at least some kind of timescale.

The counselling interview: summary checklist
1. Preparation:
   Quiet location
   Be generous with time
2. Structure:
   Establish trust
   Identify and explore the problem
   Help the interviewee reach a solution
3. Deal with the emotion first.
4. Use active listening.
5. Separate:
   Symptoms
   Causes
   Solutions
6. Clarify, probe, and reflect back.
7. Confront, but only when you can be specific.
8. Summarize each interview at the time.
9. Follow up each interview.

6
The grievance interview

There are three main problems facing you at the start of a grievance interview:

- Preparation
- Emotion
- Clarification.

Someone bearing a grievance may arrive on your doorstep with little or no warning. As with the counselling interview, they might not be prepared to tell you about the matter in advance, so the chances of doing any preparation are often strictly limited. In all of the other chapters in this book, the importance of good preparation has been emphasized. What preparation can be done in this case?

Preparation

Although someone may not want to warn you in advance that they have a grievance, it is quite likely that they will have told someone else at work. Part of your responsibility as a manager is to keep in touch with what's going on. As the management book *In Search of Excellence* puts it, 'managing by wandering about' is the thing to do.

You may have heard some rumblings, and it may be possible to make some discreet enquiries. At this stage, it is worth gathering facts and opinions. But make sure that you know which are which. When you get on to the clarifying part of the process, it will not help if you are basing your questions on an assumption that turns out to be false. Even so, some kind of preparation will probably repay you enormously when one of your staff comes to you with a complaint.

If life were straightforward and totally logical, the person with the complaint would explain clearly and simply what the problem was, you would both discuss it, find a mutually agreeable solution and that would be it. However, life isn't like that. If it were, the need for managers would be much reduced! Very often, the person with the complaint is pretty steamed up about it. So before you can get on to solving the problem, you will have to go through two other stages.

Emotion

In most instances a person with a grievance is angry. Angry with you, the company, working colleagues, or some combination of these. Of course other emotions will be brought to you as well, but anger seems to be the most common.

The same general principles apply here as in the counselling interview. You must deal with the emotion before you can get on to the problem-solving part of the discussion. Your long-term relationship with the person you are seeing is most important here. If they know you can be trusted, then you can probably expect them to listen to you now, even though things may look bad from their point of view. If you don't know the person well, then you must expect to take quite a time to build up some kind of working relationship.

At first you may just have to let the person blow off steam. They may be clear and coherent, or they may be very muddled. Whatever happens, don't get into arguments and counter-accusations at this stage. This is especially important if you have been able to do some homework, and have your own thoughts about why the person is seeing you. While someone is angry they will not be able to have a rational discussion with you. If you get angry too, then you'll just be delaying the time when you can get down to the facts of the problem.

Before we leave this section, I ought to mention that some managers find that having rows at work is sometimes helpful in 'clearing the air' before getting on with solving the problem. Personally, I don't like that approach, since I feel that losing your temper is a bit like losing some of your sense. Running organizations is hard enough anyway, without cutting yourself off from all of your abilities. I entirely agree that there is often a need to blow off steam, but I'd much rather do that with people that I'm not potentially in conflict with. Losing your temper for effect is all very well if you can ration yourself, but if it becomes an act, or worse still a spectator sport, then you are digging a managerial bear-trap for yourself.

Clarifying

One way or another you have got through the emotional stage. Now you need to ask the question:

What is the real grievance?

It sounds like a simple matter and for some it is, but quite a lot of people seem to dislike approaching a problem directly. Your job will be to clarify and confirm with the person precisely what the problem is, and then to move on to finding an equitable solution.

Start off with some open questions. Anyone coming to you will probably have their story already worked out. Persuade your interviewee to talk and ask clarifying questions as you go. If they have only just cooled down from the previous section then don't interrupt too much, otherwise anger may erupt again. Towards the end of the clarifying process you will probably need to ask some fairly specific closed questions to establish precise facts. There may be some disagreement, and it will be useful to establish who else could back up the evidence.

At convenient breaks in the conversation, summarize the story as you have understood it so far. These little summaries needn't take more than a few seconds, but are very useful in preventing you going on too long with a misunderstanding. With a little practice it is possible to include these summaries as part of your listening and questioning style. It is not the kind of style you would use all the time, but it is very appropriate during the listening phase of several kinds of interview and meeting.

Your style during this stage of the interview will need to give at least some control to the interviewee. They will need to tell the story in their own words, and largely in their own time. You can of course try to keep to the point, but until you have heard the story you are not able to judge what that point is. As with the counselling interview, you may not like to give away this amount of control, but it will probably be faster overall. It will depend on how defensive you feel.

The grievance may well have implications about you and your style as a manager. It may just be, Oh Exalted One, that you don't want to hear anything that might come over as critical. You wouldn't be alone in this. So there may also be a temptation to discourage the person from telling you everything they think about the problem, because part of that thought process is going to be critical of you. Fight the temptation. Wouldn't you rather be the first to know, or would you prefer that your boss heard first? At least if there is something that you could improve on, you will be able to do something about it. If the message gets back to you by a different route there may be fewer options left.

People can indicate in all kinds of ways that they really don't want to listen. If you are doing that during a grievance interview, then you are probably not getting all the facts, and certainly not all the opinions. Your voice tone, your body language, your sense of urgency or priority, will all give messages to the person you are talking to. If those messages say you aren't interested, then in some way or another, you'll be repaid in kind.

The interview
You have done what preparation you can. The person has come in and sat down. You have asked an open question to get things rolling. It turns out that the person is not particularly worked up about the problem, but very definitely wants something done. You move onto the clarifying stage. You let the person talk, ask a few questions to clarify, then summarize what you have heard. You agree the summary. Now two of you know what the person sees as the problem. You have yet to state your views or involve anyone else.

Problems you can solve
At this stage there are a lot of options. If you feel that the grievance is genuine and can be solved on the spot, then get on with it. It may be that there is a genuine grievance which can't be dealt with straight away. You will need to discuss how the grievance could be handled. The solution may involve someone else, who may need to be convinced that they need to change their ways. Here it is important to avoid making promises that you can't keep. If the complaint is against someone else, then you should at least give that other person a chance to explain their part. Your role is not to take sides, but to make sure that your staff are treated fairly. However much you side with or against the complaint, the other people in the argument must be given a chance.

This is harder if the company rules or conditions are the subject of the complaint. You are the person's boss, but you are also a representative of the company. Both sides in this dual role may be in conflict, and although your job is still to find a fair solution, other people will find it hard to believe that you acted impartially if you give them cause to doubt your fairness. A technique that is often used here is the hypothetical situation. For example:

What would happen to the work load if everyone were treated in the way you are asking the company to treat you?

or

> How would you feel if you were Ann, and I'd complained about you in this way? How would you want to solve this problem?

Hypothetical situations must be treated carefully, since it's easy to lose sight of reality quite quickly. But as a way of creating new solutions, or loosening up old solutions, the technique can be very helpful.

Problems you can't solve
There will be grievances for which you have no solution. In such cases the person will have to learn to live with what they have got. Hypothetical questions may help them to realize that what they want is impractical, but sometimes you are going to be tempted to say something along the lines of, 'if you don't like it you'd better go and look elsewhere'. Such temptations could well be rewarded with a constructive dismissal case, so don't express yourself too freely on the matter.

You may need to state company policy on the subject, so make sure that you have copies of rule books or policy statements to hand. If you have a procedure that goes beyond this point, then you should inform the person of what has to be done to take their complaint on to the next stage. You should also inform anyone else who will be affected by the next stage in the grievance procedure.

The record
Whatever the result of the interview, always summarize fully at the end, and always make a note of the main points and the actions to be taken. A written record will be important if the complaint goes further. It will also be a useful action plan to chart the progress of any remedial action that you or others are going to take. Make sure that the complainant gets a copy of the written record.

Follow up any action that has to be taken, and fix a review meeting with the complainant at a suitable date in the future to check that all is well.

An example—A grievance interview
Fred Naylor is the production manager of a small electronic engineering company. Joan Terry is the supervisor of the wiring section, and is one of four supervisors in the production department. She is the only woman supervisor. Two days after Joan's return from holiday she has told Fred

that she wants to see him about something, but won't say what it is about.

FD: 'Come in Joan, please sit down. What do you want to see me about?'

JT: 'Well, it's not really about the work, it's more about me. You see I feel that I have been doing good work over the last few years, and the company has expanded which has put a lot more work through the wiring section, and yet I think I'm still treated as the most junior of the supervisors. Sometimes almost as if I'm not a proper supervisor at all.'

FD: 'Joan, that surprises me, you are one of our more experienced supervisors. Can you be more specific and give me some examples of how you feel you are being treated as the most junior?'

Comment: Joan has not made herself very clear. Fred's first job is to try to clarify what she is unhappy about. He has been careful not to rush onto the defensive and deny that she is treated the way she says she is. There is no point in arguing about the facts at this stage because they have not yet emerged.

JT: 'It's hard to give examples, because I think it is the attitude that the other supervisors have. They seem to treat me and the wiring section as the least important. I sometimes feel that it's you four men who run production, and then you tell the women, who get on with the work.'

FN: 'That's a fairly tough criticism, Joan. And it's certainly not my intention that this department should be run like that. My aim is that each supervisor should have an equal say in the running of this department. Can you give me an example of something that has happened recently to make you feel that the men have more influence?'

Comment: Joan still hasn't produced any evidence, so Fred keeps trying to get her to give examples. Until they have something concrete to discuss there is little point in trying to go on to the problem-solving stage. Fred knows that Joan isn't given to flights of fancy, that there must be something that is making her feel that she is not being treated fairly.

JT: 'Well, I notice that all the other supervisors have been given dates for going on the supervisors' training course, whereas I don't even know if I'm going. I know that some of the other supervisors are young men with longer careers in front of them, but even so, I don't see why I shouldn't go as well.'

Comment: At last! Some information. If Fred was intending to send Joan on the course, then he has slipped up by not telling her. But is that all? Is there more to Joan's complaint?

FN: 'Joan, I'm very sorry about that, yes of course you are going to go on the same course as the others, but I'm afraid that with the holiday season I wanted to be able to see you before fixing a date. But is that really what was bothering you?'

Comment: Fred has admitted his mistake, and has asked if there is something more serious, without implying that Joan was getting upset over something trivial. To Joan, it might not have been trivial.

JT: 'Yes, there is something else. I was very upset that you waited until I was on holiday to make changes in the work rotas. It seemed to me that as soon as I was out of the way on holiday, you and the others got together and agreed new schedules without thinking of involving me, or considering my section.'

FN: 'What changes have you found in the rotas which affect your section?'

JT: 'There aren't many. But that's not the point. Why did you wait until I was away before making any changes?'

Comment: The complaint seems to be that Joan was not consulted, rather than the changes themselves.

FN: 'Look, I appreciate that you should have been involved in the changes, and normally you would have been, but we did have an urgent problem to cope with and the only way I could see of handling it was to change the schedules. I'm at fault for not telling you about it the moment you came back from your holiday, and I apologize for that. Because there was little effect on your section, I let it slip to the back of my mind. But I am still worried that you feel you are not being involved enough. This incident has brought that out quite clearly. What can we both do to improve things?'

Comment: Fred has been prepared to admit guilt when he sees that Joan has a real grievance. But he is also concerned that this particular complaint may be a symptom of a bigger problem. He would like to use this opportunity to make working relations more positive. He is deliberately adopting a problem-solving approach and asking Joan to help him with it.

JT: 'I think we need to be able to talk more. I know we have regular supervisors' meetings, but then you and the other men also meet at other times too. I don't want to have to join your cricket team or go to your pub to have a conversation, but I would like to be able to discuss what we are doing and the various problems we have.'

FN: 'Yes, I see what you mean. Although, as business develops I find myself with less and less time, and more and more to do. The other thing that worries me is that if the other three supervisors see me having meetings with you, then they are going to want the same. I think I spend too much time at meetings already, I'd like to spend less time. Have you any ideas?'

Comment: Fred is a busy person, and he is not prepared to make commitments that he knows he couldn't keep. He puts the problem back to Joan.

JT: 'Well, we could meet at lunchtime from time to time. That way we could talk informally, and it wouldn't take up any work time. Would that be possible?'

FN: 'Yes that would be fine, although, as I quite often take customers out for lunch, it would be worth us booking up our meetings in advance so that we could keep the time free. As it is a good idea, I don't want to exclude the other supervisors from it. If you don't mind I will send them all a note saying that if they want to talk to me individually, then they could also use the lunch period.'

Comment: They have reached a solution to Joan's problem. Fred is informing others who might otherwise be curious. But before they stop, Fred should do two more important things.

FN: 'Before we finish, are there any other matters that you want to raise with me? I appreciate that I have been difficult to contact, and I don't want anything else to be causing problems.'

JT: 'No, I'm happy that we have been able to talk, and I think some lunchtime meetings will help keep me in the picture.'

FN: 'Fine. Now let us summarize what we have decided. We will discuss dates for you to go on the supervisors' course. We will arrange to have occasional lunchtime meetings to help keep us both up to date on what is going on. I have said that I regard all my supervisors as having an equal responsibility for contributing to the effectiveness of this department, and that most definitely includes you. I hope this meeting has helped, and do please tell me if you feel that things are not right in future. I suggest that we review how these lunchtime meetings are going in three months' time. I'll put it in the diary and send you a note to remind us both.'

Comment: Fred gave Joan the opportunity to raise any further points, having established a good atmosphere with the meeting so far. He then summarized what they had agreed, and arranged for a review to see if the whole thing was working.

The grievance interview: summary checklist
1. Preparation:
     Make discreet enquiries
2. Emotion:
     Deal with this first
3. Clarification:
     Start with open questions
     What is the real grievance?
     Make brief summaries
     Encourage even the bad news
4. Solutions:
     Use hypothetical questions
     Don't make promises you can't keep
     Inform others who are involved
5. Summarize:
     In writing if appropriate
6. Follow up the action plan to ensure it happens.

7
The disciplinary interview

There are two distinct types of disciplinary interview. There is the formal sort, where the powers that be (this may mean you) have put the disciplinary machine into motion and are looking for the swiftest way to get rid of the individual concerned. At the other end of the scale there may be all kinds of informal meetings where, although you do not want to lose a particular member of the staff, it is important that that person recognizes the need to improve rapidly.

As with any interview, preparation beforehand is important. With disciplinary interviews it is essential that you know in your own mind which kind of interview you are going to run. The style you use, the number of other people involved, the timing and the notes you write afterwards will all be affected.

Preparation
Depending on the severity of the offence and the stage of the procedure that you have reached, this meeting could be quite momentous in the life of the interviewee. It is therefore very important that you have checked your facts and are quite clear on what the problem is. If this meeting has happened after a series of written warnings then there will be a quantity of paperwork to check. Comments will have been made to you before the event, some of them factual, others just opinions. Your role will be to separate fact from opinion and to translate those messages so that both the interviewee and the company get a fair deal.

Procedure
This may be an informal five-minute chat, or it may be a major production, stage-managed from either side. You need to know. You need to have checked your company's discipline procedure and to have

asked around for guidance on precedents. It is also important to find out what the next stage in the formal system will be.

If you have little or no procedure, then think the thing through with a colleague. Half-way through the interview is no place to start trying to invent policy.

Punishments and sanctions

After reviewing procedure, look carefully at what action you could take. This may range from doing nothing, to sacking. If you have a procedure, then it may well give you some guidance. With no guidance available, consider whether you want the punishment to fit the crime, or to fit the person, or just to limit the damage. If you believe that there is hope for the person, then you will want to set targets for performance or behaviour that will lead back to the standards of performance that you expect of all your staff. If you believe that there is no hope, then you are likely to be choosing options which limit any further damage that the person can do. This might be a move to other kinds of work, or a different part of the business, or less freedom with time, money or other resources.

At the interview you will let the interviewee have an opportunity to give their point of view. Some new evidence may emerge at this time. It is important that you should be able to adjust your final decision to take this new evidence into account. Don't make up your mind before the event. Do make sure that the range of actions you will choose from are actually possible. This is especially important if your organization has disciplinary procedures and codes.

Unfair dismissal

There is, of course, legislation to prevent unfair and wrongful dismissal. It is to be hoped that your selection, appraisal and grievance methods are coping with most of your staff management problems, and you don't spend all of your time throwing staff out of your company. However, if you do need to sack someone, make sure that you have checked your thinking through with someone else, and that you are not setting yourself up for an obvious unfair dismissal case. You may still be taken to a tribunal, but if you have prepared your ground well, followed a consistent course, and given the aggrieved person reasonable opportunities to explain their point of view and, if appropriate, to correct the problem, then you must stand a reasonably good chance at the tribunal hearing.

The interview that results in someone being sacked is unlikely to involve much trust on either side. It is typical for the manager to adopt a formal controlled style that has the least chance of 'giving away' anything. This is the only type of interview for which it may be worth writing out some statements in advance. By comparison with the other interviews described in this book, it is scarcely an interview at all. Very little exchange of ideas or information goes on, and very often the outcome is already decided.

I should like to spend most of the rest of this chapter looking at the kind of disciplinary interview in which there is some hope that the employee can actually make some changes. In this instance the effectively managed interview can be the first step on the road to good performance. Let us look at the interview itself.

The interview
In the interview there will be a mixture of telling, listening, persuading and recording. The proportions of the mix will depend on your own style, the severity of the problem, and the person you are interviewing. You want an outcome from the meeting, and that must include improved performance—hopefully because the person concerned has improved.

Purpose
At the start of the interview you need to be clear on what the purpose really is. It may be to have a good shout at your employee. This will probably do you a lot of good, but it may not encourage the person to improve. If you don't explain precisely what is being done wrong, and what has to be done to improve, then how can you expect any improvement?

Another purpose might be to let the person know just how serious the problem is, and the consequences for the future. They may not have realized what the implications could be. Whatever the objectives of the interview, you need to have thought through how you will tackle each of them in a systematic and effective way. In short, you will need a plan. As part of your plan, the style you use will be very important.

Style
The more serious the interview, the more formal; and the more formal the more you are likely to want to retain control of the event. In extreme cases, where you know exactly what outcome you want and what is to be

said, then you are probably going to want to retain absolute control of the whole meeting.

In most interviews you will want to give the interviewee some opportunity to explain what they have done (or not done) and, during this part at least, you may choose to use open questions. For most of the time, however, you are going to be using varying degrees of closed question. These will establish facts, sort out precisely who did what, who was there, etc., etc. When you have sorted out this information, you may wish to move into a problem-solving style. If, for instance, the person cannot get to work on time, then it might be worth exploring methods of ensuring prompt arrival, such as buying an alarm clock, getting up earlier, getting a lift with a friend, an earlier train. . . . If the cause of the trouble turns out to be a personal or domestic problem you could end up using a counselling style which leads into a problem-solving approach. If that does happen, do be careful that the interviewee takes on responsibility for making whatever changes are necessary to bring about an improvement. Don't encourage dependency.

On some occasions, it will be difficult, but do try to keep calm. The disciplinary interview that turns into a ding-dong slanging match may well let off some steam, but it probably won't help you achieve your purpose very effectively. In the heat of the moment you may say something that will later prove to be a hindrance to you making your case. This is especially true if the interviewee has a representative present.

Having assessed the problem and found ways to tackle it, you now need to ensure that it actually gets tackled: you need an action plan.

Action plan
Keep a detailed record of what was discussed and the action that was agreed at the end. The action plan should include ways of measuring progress, and very often further meetings to review that progress. Dates, times, and performance measures should be recorded and a copy given to the interviewee as soon as possible after the interview. If you are nearing the end of the disciplinary process, then a statement of the consequences of not meeting the targets in the plan should also be included. At the end of the interview, you MUST SUMMARIZE. This is important for two reasons: first as a check that the interview has covered all the points; second as confirmation of the action plan.

Some kind of follow-up must be built into the action plan. The follow-up may be done by you, or it may be done by other managers or supervisors. If others are involved then they must also receive a copy of the action plan.

An example—A disciplinary interview
Jane Peters is the management accountant for a clothing retailer. Her assistant, Alan Waterman, has been producing work which is below his usual standard. It is sometimes late and frequently has too many mistakes. Jane has mentioned individual examples to Alan, but now feels that a proper meeting is called for.

JP: 'Alan, you have worked for me for the last two years and your work has normally been of a high standard. Recently I have had to pick you up on trivial errors, and a couple of times in the last month you have been late with the weekly figures. This isn't your normal standard of work, what's going wrong?'

Comment: Jane is recognizing the good work that Alan has done in the past, to contrast against his present performance. She asks him an open question about the present.

AW: 'Well, I'm sorry, but we have been under a lot of pressure recently. We do seem to get a lot of extra requests for special reports. And when they come from the board you have to drop everything to give them what they want.'

JP: 'Yes, I understand that, but it still seems unlike you to let work go that has not been thoroughly checked. Is there anything else that might be affecting your work?'

Comment: Jane guesses that Alan's reply is fobbing her off, so she probes harder.

AW: 'I do feel I've got a lot on at the moment. The work load here seems to be increasing and I'm also just coming up to my final stage accountancy exams. Although I've done quite a lot of preparation, I do find myself worrying about them.'

Comment: So now we may be getting somewhere. Has Alan got too many other things on his mind—like the forthcoming exams? Also, can he handle a variety of work coming at him from several directions? Jane decides to check this out.

JP: 'What do you feel has increased over, say, the last three months?'

AW: 'It's difficult to put my finger exactly on it. There just seems to be more to do. I don't think that it comes from any particular source.'

Comment: Nothing too clear from that. Perhaps a more direct approach might work.

JP: 'So it's not any one person or department that is asking for more. . . I'm wondering what else it might be. How much do you think that your exams are affecting your work?'

AW: 'Not at all, I hope. But I suppose if I were honest, they have been bothering me, and I'm doing some revision during the lunch hour. Perhaps sometimes I carry on thinking about the revision material after lunch.'

Comment: It's either a skilful hoax, or Jane really has uncovered the reason for the change in performance. If the latter, she must now explain the seriousness of the problem, and look for a way to help Alan solve his own problem.

JP: 'We can look at ways to help you prepare for your exams in a moment, but first I want to make sure you appreciate the importance of you producing good work of high accuracy. Obviously the company needs to do its management accounting effectively, since many of the major decisions taken by the board will be based on data supplied by you. Remember that they know who does what in this place. I act as a filter, but good work is seen as coming from the entire team, not just me. Senior managers will be keen to recognize quality and to reward it. Equally, they will not tolerate poor work for long, and passing your exams will be no substitute for a poor track record. So, bear in mind that failing to perform well can have serious effects in the short and the long term. Do you appreciate that?'

AW: 'I hadn't really thought about it, but I do now.'

JP: (Adopting a rather less serious tone) 'So what can we do about these exams? Is it basic knowledge you need, or practice with the techniques?'

Comment: Jane has read Alan the riot act, and made sure that he has acknowledged the seriousness. Now she has moved on to some joint problem-solving.

AW: 'It's really the practice. I work through the examples, but some of them seem rather remote from my own experience.'

JP: 'Well, perhaps we could find you some work here that would allow you to practice the techniques, but on material that you are familiar with. I'm sure that we could also rope in some of the other financial people to provide examples. If you don't mind doing some of this in your own time, then I expect they would be only too pleased to give you some short projects to work on. In return you could ask them to talk you through your results. Would that help?'

Comment: Jane might have offered time off, but obviously didn't feel this was possible. She has not mentioned it and has moved into areas which might be of help.

They now discuss what sort of examples and techniques Alan wants to practice. Having done that, Jane summarizes.

JP: 'Alan, I want you to pass your exams, but I also expect you to work to a consistently high standard. You must not let your preparation get in the way. I hope that we have now worked out a way to help you help us. I would like to review your work with you in two weeks' time (they fix a date and time then) and I'm expecting to see you back on track with the accuracy and time-keeping. In the meantime, do let me know if I can help. It's a while since I sat my exams but I expect that I can still remember some of it.'

The disciplinary interview: summary checklist
1. Preparation:
    Which stage in the procedure?
    What sanctions are available?
    What is your aim for the outcome?
2. The interview:
    Style appropriate to purpose
    Gather the facts
    Listen to opinions
    Try to keep calm
    Draw up an action plan
    Summarize
3. Follow-up:
    Check progress against action plan
    Praise success

8
Information giving and gathering

Most of the interviews described in this book are designed to achieve one specific purpose. We have looked at selection, appraisal, counselling, etc. In this chapter I want to look at the range of meetings that often occur between two people where there may not be quite such a clear purpose for the meeting. In this context I am going to use the terms interview and meeting to mean the same thing. Some examples are:

- *The exit interview*. To discover why someone is leaving and what can be learned from their resignation.
- *The consultancy interview*. One person has some expertise which the other person wants to make use of. The client needs advice on an unfamiliar subject, the consultant knows the subject, but does not know the client's particular needs.
- *The research interview*. The interviewer wants to find out information, or the opinions of a number of people, and is seeing them on an individual basis. The interviewer may have to write up a report of the findings.
- *The technical briefing*. Here a specialist is briefing another specialist in their own field. The main concern of both parties is to ensure accuracy and a very high level of understanding.

The linking feature between all these meetings will be that the interviewer (the person who called the meeting) may not know which aspects of the meeting will be important to the interviewee. So, unlike most of the other interviews described, it may be difficult to forecast in advance what subject areas will need to be covered and to what depth. There is an added complication, which is that in some cases the interviewee may want to give you lots of information that you do not need. Part of your task in conducting the interview is to learn what is important and what is not.

Preparation
From what has already been said, it is clear that preparation will not be straightforward. So, start with the information you have. Why have you called this meeting? What would be the best possible outcome? It may be that, as the result of this meeting, a problem you have is solved. Fine, so what would that mean? Would it mean that you weren't involved with the problem anymore, or that you now knew how to handle it, or that you could hand it over to someone else? Whatever it is, if you think about it you must have some idea what a satisfactory outcome for the interview would be. So jot down your best outcomes for the meeting.

Now jot down what you don't want to happen. It could be that you find out nothing new, or that you are given wrong information, or that you are given information that you cannot understand. There are probably lots of possible bad outcomes, some less likely than others. However, the point about them all is to ask yourself just two questions.

1. How will I know (that the interview is going wrong)?
2. How will I stop it happening?

For example, in a research interview about customer preferences, your best outcome might be to find out exactly which products the customer was keen to buy and at what price. The worst outcome might be to fail to get the customer to talk about that particular kind of product at all. A way of stopping this worst outcome might be to prepare several questions about the product range.

So, although it may not be possible to prepare in quite the same way as with other interviews, preparation is essential. That preparation will include consideration of whether time or place are important to the success of the interview.

Timing
The exit interview conducted in the staff car park after the farewell booze-up is probably going to be fairly entertaining—especially for any onlookers—but is unlikely to provide much useful information. Of course there are times when the leaver, strengthened by the occasion, may reveal some previously hidden fact or prejudice which may explain the departure of staff. But if things are that bad, then the cause of the

problem is unlikely to want to listen anyway—especially if it's you, and you just feel you have been insulted by what has been said.

Timing is therefore important. An exit interview should not be done in a rush on the last day. If you are asking a consultant to advise you, or if you are trying to advise someone else, don't try to cram everything into a 20-minute walk round the factory. When neither of you knows how much the other does not know, it is very easy to make assumptions about what can be left out. When things have gone wrong, the sad exchange of

Me: 'Why didn't you tell me?'

You: 'You never asked me.'

is an all too frequent reminder of what happens when not enough time is allowed for each side of the discussion to check on what the other side does and does not know.

Style

The style you use will depend largely on the kind of interview you are conducting. Where new information is being generated, the interviewer should make regular summaries of what has emerged. Note-taking will probably be more important during the interview, and the pace of the interview might be adapted to allow notes to be made.

The early stages of exit and research interviews would probably involve a lot of open questions, to get the other person talking. As specific data emerges, then more closed questions will be appropriate to clarify what is being said.

The exit interview

An employee may leave for a variety of reasons, and although that person may give a reason for going, it may not be the real reason. They may have become frustrated through poor management, or lack of opportunities for training, or some other kind of problem that was not adequately dealt with. An exit interview may even tell you something about the quality of recruitment in the company. Are you in fact getting the right people for the right job?

The preparation you can do will depend on how well you know the person who is leaving. Reasons for resignation may be included in the letter of resignation, but it would be worth talking to that person's immediate supervisor and their colleagues to see if you could find other possible reasons.

Make sure that the meeting takes place without interruptions. In order to get someone to talk openly, you will require some privacy. It may be, for instance, that the person is leaving to go to a company where a higher rate of pay is the main attraction. If that is the case, a discussion about pay will need to be confidential.

Can you win people back at exit interviews? Managers certainly try, although it seems a bit late in the day to suddenly recognize the true worth of an employee. Of course, some employees use the resignation tactic as a way of drawing attention to themselves and, sometimes, improving their pay or conditions.

If someone is leaving you, then if possible try to make the final departure a positive affair. In a small way each person is an advertisement for your organization. After all, you recruited them and trained them, so people will judge your company by what they see. If employees leave you feeling badly about the way they have been treated, then they are likely to make or imply all kinds of criticisms about the way your business works. If people belong to specialist groups from which you recruit regularly (i.e., electronics engineers), then your company's ability to recruit may be damaged.

The consultancy interview
You employ a consultant because you do not have enough specialist information or skills. If you are to work effectively together, then you must each spend some time finding out what the other knows and, just as important, what the other does not know.

If you are the client who has called in the consultant, then you may be concerned about control. You may worry that with all that expert knowledge, the consultant will blind you with science and then sell you the most expensive option. As the client you can do a lot to prevent this, by thinking through what criteria the consultant's solution will need to satisfy in order to meet your needs. You may have targets for price, timescales, ease of use, size, level of disruption, etc., etc. It is far better to have worked these out roughly for yourself. Otherwise your thinking is likely to be conditioned by what is said, not by what you want.

You will need to control the meeting to the extent that you can ask the questions that you have prepared and indicate the criteria that you want to work to. Remember that although consultants are experts in their own field, they probably don't know much about your part of the organization. Where that is concerned, you are the expert, and could just as easily blind the consultant with science. If you are concerned about control, your local knowledge gives you quite a lot of power if you want to use it.

While we are on the subject of your local knowledge, a word or two about jargon. A lot of people are worried about speaking to experts because of the jargon that they use. If you are learning about a subject that is new to you, then you will probably have to learn a few new words, but that doesn't mean that the language learning should be all one way. The expert should be just as prepared to learn some of the language that relates to your particular work. A good rule of thumb for judging experts is whether they are prepared to learn your language and translate their jargon into words that you understand.

The meeting that you have with your consultant will need to be summarized and an action plan agreed for the future, together with an agenda for the next meeting.

The research interview

Some research interviews are structured, and are based on a fixed set of questions that have to be read out to the interviewee. At the other end of the scale is the kind of interview done to gather information, ideas and opinions, to form the basis of a report and recommendations.

In the first case, virtually all the preparation has been done in advance. The interviewer's role is to ensure that members of the target population are questioned. In the second case, the interviewer will have prepared by thinking through the areas that need to be covered in the interview. Once the interview starts, the interviewer will have to listen carefully and follow up subjects that sound relevant.

Location and timing are likely to be less critical than with other interviews, unless confidential material is being discussed. The style will depend on how much the interviewer already knows about the subject. If a lot is known, then closed questions can be used, and the interview can be fairly swift. If not much is known, then open questions are going to be essential to cover a wider area, before narrowing down with closed questions.

If you are using mainly closed questions, do be very careful about the exact phrasing you use. I remember being told about a medical survey where an interviewer, following a questionnaire, asked an obviously asthmatic man, 'Do you suffer from shortness of breath when you walk upstairs?' To which he replied, 'No.' Since she felt this was a curious answer from someone who seemed to have difficulty breathing at all, the interviewer broke away from her prepared questions and asked the subject why he responded in this way. He replied that he didn't *suffer* from shortness of breath, because he always took good care to go upstairs very slowly! He had understood the question to be about how much discomfort his breathing problems caused him, rather than what his breathing problems were. He was keen to point out how much he had adapted his behaviour to cope with his medical condition.

The technical briefing
In conventional terms, this is scarcely an interview at all. But taking the definition of an interview as being a meeting with purpose, then the technical briefing certainly comes into the category.

The prime aims for this sort of meeting are:

- Accuracy
- Understanding
- Efficiency.

Just because two experts are talking there is no guarantee that each will understand the jargon of the other. There are some similarities between this sort of interview and the consultancy meeting. Both parties should find out what the other does and doesn't know. Accuracy is increased by having the receiver of the briefing summarize the content back to the speaker. In addition the speaker should encourage the listener to ask questions at any stage if there is something that is not clear.

All this is fairly straightforward and obvious, but it is quite easy for one expert to want to show off in some way to the other. What better way than to use words that demonstrate that 'I am more expert than you'. If the other expert does not want to admit ignorance, then a potentially damaging misunderstanding can occur. This is a matter of attitude, not questioning technique.

Preparation for a technical briefing should be done by both participants. This should ensure that the briefer presents material in the most efficient way possible, and that the receiver has checked what relevant knowledge is required about the subject.

Style will vary and may be quite informal, but the speaker should not try to hold on to control of the entire meeting or the listener will find it difficult to ask questions—it will seem like butting in.

An example—An exit interview

Helen King is the personnel manager of a branch of a large food retailing chain. She is seeing Pauline Langley, who has given in her resignation after seven months working mainly on the till and occasionally on one of the specialist counters. They are in Helen's office, and Helen has done her best to make sure that there will be no interruptions.

HK: 'Thank you for coming to see me, Pauline. I wanted to sort out the final paperwork with you before you go, but also to talk about why you are leaving.'

Comment: Helen has decided to go for the direct approach and has defined the purpose of the meeting very plainly. They talk about the paperwork first.

HK: 'You have been with us only seven months, and now you are resigning. You said on our leaving form that your reason for leaving was for better work. What does that mean?'

PL: 'Well, really, to work in a smaller shop.'

Comment: Helen has started off with an open question, but has not got very far with it. This looks like being an uphill task.

HK: 'What is the attraction of a smaller shop?'

PL: 'I suppose I prefer working with just a few other staff, and having more to do with customers.'

HK: 'How much do you feel you dealt with customers in this store?'

Comment: Helen is determinedly keeping to open questions, so that she hears Pauline's own view rather than a repeat of her own views.

PL: 'I was dealing with customers every day, but mainly on the till. I didn't feel that I was helping very much, just running the till, and that gets very boring.'

HK: 'What could we have done to make your job more interesting?'

PL: 'Well, I don't mind taking my share on the till, but I think some people just get sent on the till day after day. I would have liked more chance to work on the specialist food counters. I think layout makes a big difference, too. Customers want to buy fresh food that is well presented. I would have liked to work on that and learn something about layout.'

Comment: Helen's patience with open questions has paid off, and now Pauline is saying what she really thinks. Now is the time to ask her what prompted her to leave.

HK: 'I'm sure you appreciate that it's not possible to go straight onto display work within the first few months. People have to get general experience of working in the store before they can concentrate on one counter. You know all this, so what prompted you to leave now?'

PL: 'Well, I know that I'm supposed to work towards more responsibility, but some departments have favourites, and others don't like new people coming in and making suggestions about different ways of presenting the merchandise. They're all too stuck in their ways to want to change.'

Comment: Pauline seems to be bitter about her treatment. Helen must now find out how much of this is accurate, and how much is due to Pauline's bitterness.

HK: 'When you suggested new ways of presentation, what did you say?'

PL: 'Oh, I know what you're asking. Was I rude, or too pushy?'

HK: (smiling) 'Well, sometimes we can get so enthusiastic about an idea that we forget the rest of the world may need some convincing. What did you say, and, just as important, how did you say it?'

PL: 'I did try to be polite, really. I asked Mr Simmons if he had seen the fruit displays in the hypermarket on the ring road. I said I thought that kind of layout made the fruit more attractive. I asked if he would like me to have a go at rearranging our fruit display. He said he thought our display was perfectly adequate as it was. After that I never got invited back to the fruit counter.'

HK: 'Thinking back on it, does it seem a little forward to be offering to reorganize the display on your first visit to it?'

Comment: Helen is aiming to get Pauline to see that the approach she chose was at least partly the cause of her problems.

PL: 'Well, yes, I guess so. But I was trying to help, and Mr Simmons just didn't want to know.'

HK: 'Well, you have obviously got lots of ideas. I think you may need to practice selling them to people, if you don't want too many disappointments. Do you think the smaller shop will give you those opportunities?'

PL: 'I hope so. I can see that I do sometimes rush in, but I get an idea and I want to do something about it.'

HK: 'Are there any other points about the job that you would like to mention? I am always interested to hear how we can improve our recruitment or training methods.'

Comment: A general catch-all question is often useful to sweep up any other points.

PL: 'No, not really, But I have appreciated telling you about what happened to me.'

HK: 'I want to thank you for being so direct. It will help the store to find ways to encourage new ideas while at the same time balancing them against the tried and tested practices we already have. Can I wish you good luck in your new job? I hope that you can find ways to sell your ideas to your new bosses. If you can, then I think your future could be very bright.'

Comment: Always try to end on a positive note. Once this person has left you she will be seen by others as an advertisement for you.

Information giving and gathering: summary checklist
1. Preparation:
    What would be the best outcome?
    What would be the worst outcome?
2. Timing and location:
    Is confidentiality necessary?
    Realistically, how long is needed?
3. Information:
    What do I need to know?
    What does the other person need to know?
    What do we both know already?
    What jargon are we prepared to learn from each other?
4. Summarize at the end:
    Try to end an exit interview positively

9
Being an interviewee

The three key skills that apply to being an interviewer,

- Planning and preparing
- Listening and observing
- Questioning and probing

apply just as strongly to being an interviewee. Coupled to this is a fourth skill based on the expectation that you will be asked to give information about yourself or about what you have done or seen or know. This fourth skill is that of giving information in such a way that the interviewer can understand and use it as easily as possible. You must avoid falling into one of the twin traps of taking too long and giving too much detail, or being too brief and leaving out something important.

Planning and preparation
Pardon me for asking you such a direct and apparently simple question, but what is the purpose of the interview that you are about to attend? Is it a final interview to select between you and two or three other candidates? Is it a preliminary sounding by a potential client who may want to make use of your goods or services? Will you be asked to provide evidence, facts, opinions or ideas? What will you be expected to know? How long will you have? The more questions you can ask yourself (and attempt to answer) before you get to the interview, the less you will be relying on your ability to 'think of something on the spot'. Because on the spot is where you will be if you haven't done enough preparation.

Listening and observing
As the interviewee, it is likely that you are at the interview so that you can talk. However, that doesn't mean that you can stop listening and observing how your words are being received. You have a message that

you wish to get across to the interviewer and the more you can learn about ways of phrasing your message so that the interviewer gets the message you are sending, rather than something else, then the more you are helping yourself.

Telling

If some parts of the story you have to tell are complex and detailed, it is worth rehearsing what you are going to say and drawing up some notes. This applies equally to going to a job selection interview, going to see a doctor, or going to an appraisal. Use your listening and observing skills to see if you are going on too long about any particular point. If in doubt, a polite, 'Would you like a general summary or rather more detail?', should clarify your position. If you have a way with words, then make it a short way rather than the bells and whistles version. The interviewer can always ask for more detail, but will be irritated if necessary to ask for less.

Questioning and probing

Most of the time this is going to be done to you, which is why your preparation is so important. However, in making your preparations prior to the interview some uncertainties or conflicting information may have emerged. At some stage during the interview you should explain that there are some questions that you would like to put. In probably the majority of interviews described in this book, the interviewee will be offered time to ask questions, but if this should turn out not to be the case, don't forget that you have some rights too. Whether the interview is with your doctor ('What will the tablets do?') or with your boss during an appraisal ('How is this conversation related to my salary increments?'), it may be important for you to know, and the only way to find out is to ask.

Now let us look at an example from the interviewee's point of view. It is perhaps the most agonized-over interviewee role—that of going for a job.

Being interviewed for a job

You have been invited to a company for a first interview. The company has already received a completed application form from you which asked for fairly comprehensive factual information about your previous career moves including dates and salaries, but did not ask you for your opinions on what you did well or badly, etc. You have OF COURSE kept a copy of the application form you completed. What kind of preparation can you do? It probably falls into two broad categories. You will want to know about the job and the company, they will want to know about you, whether you can do the job and whether you would fit into the company.

Preparation is very important
What can you find out about the company? If you have applied through an advertisement then that should give you some help. If head-hunted then the consultant will give you some background, but after that you are on your own. Use your local library. They may have a copy of *Key British Enterprises* from Dun and Bradstreet, or *Kompass* which includes directors' names. Some business libraries (try your local polytechnic business school) may keep Extel cards which include recent financial information and a commentary on the company's history. If you have access to any of the burgeoning electronic databases, then make use of them for all they are worth. However, some of the data that is now available in this country is actually stored on computers in Europe or America, so check who is going to pay the phone bill and computer search-time before commissioning anything too grandiose. There are a number of other sources of data which should not be ignored. The first is that public companies produce an annual report and chairman's statement to shareholders. A second source of information is the city page of your newspaper. Incidently, there are electronic and paper summaries of the last few years of various newspaper reports categorized by subject. It should not be too hard to find out what the most recent newspaper references to the company were. Finally, it is likely that you probably know someone who knows something about the company. Ask for views and information. So much the better if you can speak with someone who works for the company already.

In doing your research you are aiming to find out whether you could work happily in that organization, what their future prospects are, and to provide yourself with some useful questions to ask the interviewer. . . 'I notice that you have moved into retailing in the last two years, how important is that to the company?' The level of research that you need to do will depend to some extent on the kind of job that you have applied for. Someone applying for a sales job is unlikely to get very far without at least some knowledge of the product range they would be expected to sell, and preferably the area or market in which they would be operating. By contrast someone else applying to the same company for a job in the finance department might be excused for having less product knowledge, although even here the accountant might be expected to know something of the accounting conventions in this particular kind of business.

So now you have an idea of what the company does and, if you are lucky, you also know something about what it would be like to work there. You have formed some thoughts about the organization's future and have still decided to go ahead with the interview. It sounds like a formality to decide at this stage to still go ahead—and in most cases it is—but do remember you always have the option of pulling out. If what you have learned so far strongly puts you off the idea of working for that organization then why waste everyone's time? Of course if you have some unanswered questions—suspicions even—then the only way to resolve them is to go to the interview and ask some direct questions. Just the same as the good interviewer will do to you!

What will they want to know about you?

As we discussed in the selection and assessment chapters, the interviewer will probably be interested in two things:

- Looking at your aptitude to do the job.
- Looking at you as a person, to find out how well you would fit into the organization.

Take aptitude first. A method I find useful is to think through the interview putting myself in the position of the interviewer. What sort of questions would I ask to find out if the candidate really does have the aptitude to take on the job? Starting there, I can ask myself as the interviewee a whole series of questions. What evidence can I quote to show that I have already been successful at part or all of the job? How might other parts of my previous experience be relevant to this particular job? What haven't I got direct experience in, and what could I offer as backup material to demonstrate that I could still do the job? In short, the more you can think like the interviewer and anticipate the questions you might be asked, the more you can spend time preparing answers that show you off to best advantage. But a word of warning here. Never be tempted to claim knowledge or skills that you don't really have. At best you may get shown up badly because the interviewer may be able to test you and you'll look silly. At worst, your application may go through to a job offer which could be withdrawn if it subsequently turns out that you made some kind of false claim at the interview. And if by then you have handed in your resignation from your previous job, then you're going to look more than silly!

How is the interviewer going to find out about you the person? It's likely to be in a number of ways, and I discussed the business of assessment of personality in Chapter 2. However, bear in mind that the interviewer, like all human beings, will be making his or her mind up about you from the moment you first walk into the room. Research in Europe and North America has shown that the interviewer will form an opinion of you somewhere between 30 and 120 seconds after first seeing you. For the more naive interviewer the rest of the interview is spent in finding ways of justifying that first opinion. Now this may not be fair, but it seems to be true. So the lesson you must take is to present a good image at the very beginning. How you dress, how you walk, how you smile, how you shake hands, are all very important to some interviewers. Without inside knowledge you should assume they are important to this interviewer. Indeed, in America a study has been made recently about how people dress and the impression which the colour and style of the clothes worn will give.

An example—Excerpts from a selection interview
The interviewer is Bob Mason, area sales manager, the interviewee is Peter Jones, applying for a sales representative's job. Bob has come out of his office to welcome Peter, they have shaken hands and Peter is now ushered into Bob's office.

BM: 'Come in Peter, sit yourself down, did you have any trouble finding us?'

Comment: Bob is trying to put Peter at ease, and is really making polite conversation. He doesn't expect a blow-by-blow account of Peter's journey, and wouldn't thank him for using up too much time with an answer at this stage.

PJ: 'No problem at all. With my present company I have made a number of calls in this area, and last year I visited your Mr Jackson to try to sell him one of our new integrated gobbledegook machines.'

Comment: Peter is anticipating that as a sales rep, one of Bob's concerns will be whether he knows the area. By answering in this sort of way he is helping Bob to appreciate early on that Peter has worked in the area. It also sounds good to be able to quote the name of the person he visited, helping to build links between Peter and his prospective employer. Bob may now wish to spend a little time finding out how much Peter knows about the company, so that any research Peter has done can be put to good use early on in the interview.

BM: 'So have you had much contact with us?'

PJ: 'The only direct contact was with Mr Jackson, and when he told me about the long-term contract his department has with our competitors there wasn't much more I could do. However, I have kept in touch, and with your development into the retail market I think there might be some new possibilities for our products.'

Comment: Peter is demonstrating that he is aware of recent developments in the company, and is also showing that as a salesman he is looking out for new sales opportunities. And all this is within the magical first two minutes of the interview.

(Bob has outlined the job to Peter and set the scene for the interview. He now wants to assess Peter's aptitude for the job. Bob is the kind of bloke who wants to get on with the job in hand and doesn't want to waste time by beating around the bush. He asks a typically direct question.)

BM: 'Tell me why you think you'd be able to do this job?'

Comment: From Peter's point of view it is a good question, since it allows him to present his strengths in the way he would like. His preparation should have covered him for this, and he ought to have rehearsed his answer to the stage where it is fluent. But before launching into too mighty a speech, it might be worth explaining to Bob what sort of format Peter has in mind. In effect Peter is making a sales presentation of himself, and most good presenters give the audience a plan for the presentation, such as:

PJ: 'I think my present job has prepared me quite well to take on the job you are advertising, so I'd like to talk about that first. Then, perhaps I could mention some points from the earlier part of my career.'

or

PJ: 'Most of my work has been in commercial sales, where of course there are different products and different customer requirements. However, I think there are a number of similarities between commercial and domestic sales which I'd like to outline to you.'

Comment: It may be that Peter's most recent experience is not in the same line as the job advertised. In this case, if he anticipates Bob's inevitable question he can answer it in his own way—which should be easier. This part of the interview is of great importance since a person's career record is quite reasonably taken to be a good predictor of how well that person will do in another job. Bob probably has some idea of the kind of answer that he is expecting, both in terms of content and in terms of detail and length. Peter's preparation will have provided the content, but there is nothing wrong in him checking with Bob just how much detail he is expecting.

PJ: (part way through his answer) 'I'm responsible for five major product lines, which range from the basic domestic mini-de-gook, up to the large industrial geiga-gook. How much would you like me to say about my selling activities for each of these?'

Comment: Bob's answer may also indicate how much control he feels he must have in the interview. Some interviewers find it hard to keep quiet for more than a sentence or two, others are quite happy to point the interviewee in the right direction and let them get on with it. If Peter is to 'come over' well at the interview it is important that Bob feels that the interview has gone well. If he feels that he has spoken too much or too little, then Bob will be less happy with the interview and most probably will feel less happy with Peter. They both need to recognize each other's needs and accomodate them if the interview is to continue in a positive way.

(Having gone through Peter's career history, Bob is now trying to assess what sort of person Peter is, and whether he would fit into the sales team. He knows that many of the current sales people will have opportunities to move into sales management, marketing, or more general management, and he wants to find out Peter's thoughts for the future. He uses an old standby.)

BM: 'If you were to join us, where do you see your career leading in the next five or ten years?'

Comment: Although an old chestnut, this is still a good question with lots of pitfalls for the unprepared. Too quick an answer and you risk sounding flippant; too modest an answer and you risk sounding like an unambitious plodder; too sharp an answer and you risk frightening Bob that his own job may be in danger in year or two; too vague an answer and you sound as if you don't think. Generally speaking, the interviewer will be looking for some signs of ambition, especially in younger people. Also, some evidence that the candidate has thought about the future, even if he/she hasn't reached any definite conclusion.

PJ: 'Eventually I should like to move into more general management, so I don't see myself staying in a sales job for all of my career. I have enjoyed the occasions when I have been able to work closely with the design and production people in my present company, and at some stage I would like the chance to broaden my experience into a more technical area.'

Comment: Peter isn't saying 'I want a specific job', but he is demonstrating that he has ambition, which is based on some previous experience.

or

PJ: 'When I was a lot younger, I worked in a variety of shopfloor and office jobs. I now realize that sales and marketing is the right area for me. I would hate to lose touch with the customer. But I don't think that means that I have to stagnate, and I think there could be a wide range of jobs that have selling in them even if they aren't as a rep. For instance I would like to manage a sales team, and possibly have a go at sales training.'

Comment: All of which gives Bob some idea of how Peter is thinking about his future, and also provides Bob with a number of possible follow-on questions.

But how does Bob get an impression of Peter as a person? There are probably as many ideas on this as there are interviewers. Some try the surprise or unusual question:

BM: 'What do you do if you can't get what you want?'

Comment: This is not a technique that I find particularly effective, but some interviewers do use it. If Peter has been listening to the kind of questions that Bob has thrown at him, then he should have some idea of what Bob is trying to find out. In that case it may well be best to reply in a way that answers the question that he feels Bob is really asking.

PJ: (they have been talking about working with other departments) 'I generally don't give in too easily, but I do tend to weigh up the value of getting what I want against the cost of getting it. If persuading a department to produce a special item for a relatively small customer would put my good relationship with that department in jeopardy, then

I would think twice about pushing too hard. A sale is one thing, but a good working relationship is probably more important in the longer term.'

Comment: Peter guesses that Bob's surprise question was prompted by the discussion on influencing other departments. Put more bluntly, it could have been phrased, 'How much of a nuisance do you make of yourself to other departments?' Peter obviously felt that it would be important to explain his concern for working closely with other departments. Bob may also want to explore Peter's ideas on some hypothetical situations. As I said in the chapter on selection, the hypothetical question needs careful handling to prevent the candidate getting too much of a clue about what the interviewer regards as the 'right' answer.

BM: 'Suppose you were visiting a customer and he suddenly started to shout abuse at you about the company and its products? What would you do?'

Comment: Quite probably Bob will have a particular incident in his mind. He will compare Peter's answer against what he did—or wished he'd done.

PJ: 'It would probably depend on how well I knew that customer. If I knew that he didn't use that approach normally, I'd take him seriously and try to see if I could calm him down. Of course there are one or two people who like to use the hard man approach to see if they can shake you. I don't let it bother me, but neither do I let them waste my time.'

Comment: In dealing with the hypothetical question, Peter is careful not to include too many assumptions of his own. Where he does make assumptions, he tells Bob about them.

(The interview continues, until Bob looks up and asks)

BM: 'Now let's turn the tables, what questions have you got for me?'

Comment: There used to be a myth that it was important to always have a question to ask at this point. My personal feeling is that if you do not have a question, then it is worse to waste a person's time by manufacturing a question, than to say that all the questions you wanted to ask have already been covered in the conversation. In this particular case one question that Peter might ask is:

PJ: 'Well, no questions about the job or the organization, you've covered all the points I wanted to ask. But what happens next as far as my application is concerned?'

Comment: If you have applied for a number of jobs, then it may be important to have an estimate of how long the decision process will take. Many interviewers will tell you this as a matter of course, but it is certainly worth asking about if they don't.

The above example gives an outline of one approach to being interviewed. Obviously, your performance at the interview will depend to a large extent on the skill of the interviewer. But even if you are faced with someone who is not as skilled or as practised as you would like, your own level of preparation and practice will at least help you make the most of the event. The key to being an effective interviewee is to prepare and to anticipate, so that, in the often stressful environment of the interview itself, not all of the questions come as a complete surprise.

Being an interviewee: summary checklist
1. Plan and prepare:
    Purpose of the interview
    Information about the company and job
    Put yourself in the interviewer's place
    Rehearse
2. Listening:
    How are you being received?
    Control in the interview
3. Telling:
    Not too long, not too short
    Practise the complex parts of the story
4. Questioning and probing:
    Ask when you need to
    An interview is a two-way process

Index

Administration, 23, 24
Advertising, 14, 16
Application form, 17, 22
Appraisal, 34–46
Assessment and decision making, 2, 4
  bad decisions, cost of, 6
  discrimination, 5, 11
  final decision, 16
Attracting candidates, 14–16

Body language (*see* Non-verbal)

Confidentiality, 50
Consultancy interview, 74, 77–79
Control, 4, 26, 40, 47, 60, 77, 79, 89
Counselling, 47–57
CV, 16, 22

Definitions, 2
Dependency, 52
Describe the person, 9, 22
  culture of the organization, 11
  expectations, 9, 13
  personality, 9, 11, 12
  skills and experience, 9, 10
Disciplinary interview, 67–73
Dismissal:
  constructive, 62
  unfair, 68

Emotion, 48, 49, 59
Empathy, 50, 53
Exit interview, 8, 9, 74–77

Follow-up, 42, 70

The grapevine, 15
Graphology, 17

Grievance, 58–66

Head-hunters, 14, 15

Information giving and gathering, 74–82
Interviewee, how to be an, 83–92

Jargon, 78
Job description, 8, 9

Listening and observing, 2, 3, 49, 60, 83, 84

Networks, 15
Non-verbal, 3, 49, 51, 53
Note-taking, 26

Panel interviews, 18
Performance standards, 37, 38
Person specification (*see* Describe the person)
Planning and preparing, 2, 8, 37
  interview plan, 22, 25
  interview structure, 39
Playing games, 24
Problem-solving, 41, 70

Questioning and probing, 2, 3, 51, 84
  closed questions, 4, 70, 78
  hypothetical questions, 4, 22, 23, 32, 40, 91
  lists of questions, 22, 25, 77
  open questions, 3, 4, 25, 70, 78
  question technique, 3

Rapport, 24
  (*see also* Empathy)

Records, 62
Research interview, 74, 75, 78, 79

Selection:
    need to fill vacancies, 7
    recruitment, 6–33
Shortlisting, 17
Style, 4, 26, 40, 67, 69, 76
    room layout, 24

stress in the interview, 12
Summary, 27, 41, 62, 70

Technical briefing, 74, 79
Tests and inventories, 18, 19
Time and timing, 23–25, 75
Training needs, 40
Trust, 49–51, 69